ILLINOIS

ILLINOIS BY ROAD

CELEBRATE THE STATES
ILLINOIS

Marlene Targ Brill

BENCHMARK BOOKS

MARSHALL CAVENDISH
NEW YORK

Benchmark Books
Marshall Cavendish Corporation
99 White Plains Road
Tarrytown, New York 10591-9001

Library of Congress Cataloging-in-Publication Data
Brill, Marlene Targ.
Illinois / by Marlene Targ Brill.
p.   cm. — (Celebrate the states)
Includes index.
Summary: Surveys the geography, history, economy, people, and state highlights of Illinois.
ISBN 0-7614-0113-X (lib. bdg.)
1. Illinois—Juvenile literature. [1. Illinois.] I. Title. II. Series.
F541.3.B74 1997   917.73—dc20   96-1879   CIP   AC

Maps and graphics supplied by Oxford Cartographers, Oxford, England

Photo research by Ellen Barrett Dudley

Cover photo: *Photo Researchers*, Adam Jones

The photographs in this book are used by permission and through the courtesy of: *Photo Researchers:* Adam Jones, 13; G. P. A. Healy, 35 (left); Porterfield Chickering, 46; John Spragens Jr., 48-49; Paul Shambroom, 62; Lawrence Migdale, 68-69; Nelson Morris, 112. *Daybreak Imagery:* Richard Day, 6-7, 15, 20, 81, 123, 124, 129, 130, 139; Todd Fink, 16, 126. *Randall Hyman:* 10-11, 58. *The Image Bank:* Ira Block, 18; Santi Visalli, 116, Tim Bieber, 119. *The Illinois State Museum:* 24-25. *The National Geographic Society:* 27. *Corbis-Bettmann:* 28, 39, 76, 90, 110, 131, 133. *Bishop Hill Historic Site:* 30. *Raymond Bial:* 31, 82, back cover. *National Museum of American Art, Washington DC/Art Resource NY:* 33. *Illinois State Historical Library:* 35 (right). *UPI/Corbis-Bettmann:* 43, 79, 98, 100 (right), 101, 103, 132, 134 (top), 136 (top and bottom), 137 (top and bottom). *AP/Wide World Photos:* 52, 54, 78, 86-87. *Odyssey/Chicago:* 56, 67, 72, 104. *Illinois Department of Commerce and Community Affairs, Bureau of Tourism:* 59, 96. *Hank Erdmann:* 60, 120. *The DuSable Museum:* 75. *Photofest:* 92. *Reuters/Corbis-Bettmann:* 93, 100 (left). *Omni Photo Communications:* 106-107. *Springer/Corbis-Bettmann:* 134 (bottom).

Printed in Italy

1 3 5 6 4 2

CONTENTS

ILLINOIS IS...

Illinois is amazing land . . .

"Makes me wonder if Illinois was grabbed by the neck, shook like a bottle of salad dressing, and then the shaker smiled when all the good ingredients settled at the bottom."

—television outdoorsman Babe Winkelman

. . . and strong people.

"The spirits of our ancestors rose and told us to avenge our wrongs or die. . . . Black Hawk is a true Indian." —Sauk chief Black Hawk

"The chief figure of the American West . . . is not the fringed-legginged man riding a raw-boned pony, but the sad-faced woman . . . in the same ragged sunbonnet which had crossed the Appalachians. . . .There was the seed of America's wealth—the woman in the sunbonnet."

—Quincy pioneer Christiana Homes Tillson

The land bore riches . . .

"On the very day of his [the settler's] arrival, he could put his plow into the ground."   —explorer Father Jacques Marquette

. . . and became the nation's heartland.

"There is a power in this nation greater than either the North or the South. . . .That power is the country known as the Valley of the Mississippi, . . . the heart and soul of the nation and continent."

—United States senator Stephen Douglas

Some people have looked out only for themselves.

"Politicians are . . . at least one long step removed from honest men." —state legislator Abraham Lincoln

"Everybody's out for the buck." —author Nelson Algren

Many have dedicated their lives to helping others . . .

"I gradually became convinced that it would be a good thing to rent a house in a part of the city where many . . . actual needs are found . . . " —Hull House founder Jane Addams

"We felt very strongly that wherever people are, art and culture should be."
　　　　—Mexican Fine Arts Center Museum founder Helen Valdez

. . . and take pride in their state.

"People, always the people, stubborn, bitter, beautiful in their towns and tattered farms. This is folk America, the region from which our democratic customs, industries, and arts continuously emerge." —historian Baker Brownell

Illinois is one of our nation's best-kept secrets. Few people, even those born in Illinois, realize how many treasures are hidden here: forested cliffs and mighty waters, sleepy mining towns and lively cities, superstars and country folks. These are the contrasts that make this state so special. This is the story of Illinois.

1 CROSSROADS OF AMERICA

Millions of years ago, shallow seas covered the land we call Illinois. Slowly, the waters froze into slabs of ice, or glaciers. Four different glaciers crept across the region over the next ten thousand years, grinding mountains flat and filling valleys.

When the climate warmed again, much of the earth dried. The glaciers left behind a layer of crushed rock and clay. Plant and animal remains mixed with other layers to form fertile topsoil. The ice carved a broad flat land. This fertile land, rich in mineral deposits, would draw settlers to Illinois for centuries.

FLATLANDS, FORESTS, AND CANYONS

Illinois is one of the twelve midwestern states. Indiana is its neighbor to the east; Iowa lies to the west and Wisconsin to the north. To the southwest is Missouri, and to the southeast is Kentucky. Tall, narrow Illinois reaches down into the South and up to northern regions, offering a range of climate and greenery.

Much of Illinois is flatter than any other prairie state. It was the first prairie region reached by European explorers, who were struck by its unusual beauty. French explorer Father Jacques Marquette wrote in the late 1600s: "We have seen nothing like this river [Illinois] that we enter, as regards its fertility of soil, its prairies and woods."

At the time, grasslands, or prairies, covered more than half the territory. The greatest stretches of prairie spread over the state's central and northern regions. Colorful grasses varied in height. Meadows of short yellow blades hid foxes and squirrels. Sand prairies housed gophers and badgers. And wild orchids tucked between the Indian yellow and big bluestem grasses in spring grew by summer to six feet tall. These grasses protected large numbers of bison, elk, and wolves, as well as white-tailed deer, the state animal.

"There are prairies three, six, ten or twenty leagues in length, and

Forests cut through flowering prairie grasses in the Iroquois County State Wildlife Area.

three in width surrounded by forests of the same extent; beyond these the prairies begin again," wrote Louis Jolliet, who led Marquette's expedition.

In early Illinois, trees shaded about 40 percent of the state. Unusual ribbons of hardwoods divided the mostly tall, wet grasslands into many smaller prairies. Scattered forests formed thick patches, or groves, on the open grasslands. That's why many Illinois communities, such as Long Grove and River Grove, have *grove* in their name.

Over time, settlers turned the rich prairies into farmland. Fults Hill Prairie and the eighteen hundred acres of Goose Lake Prairie are the only two natural grasslands now left in Illinois. Illinois is trying to restore prairie grasses and flowers in parks and along highways. Illinois poet Vachel Lindsay describes the great loss of flowered prairies:

> The tossing, blooming, perfumed grass
> Is swept away by wheat,
> Wheels and wheels and wheels spin by
> In the spring that still is sweet.
> But the flower-fed buffaloes of the spring
> Left us long ago.

Two pockets of the state escaped the crushing glaciers. In northwest Illinois, flatland turns into rolling hills with shallow valleys. White birches and mossy wetlands shelter ducks, geese, and bald eagles, our national bird. The highest point in Illinois, Charles Mound near Galena, is here.

Southern Illinois is even more surprising. Drivers heading south on Interstate 57 are amazed to see the flatland end. "The endless

Each year thousands of Canada geese fly south along the Mississippi River to hatch their goslings.

fields of corn and soybeans almost put me to sleep," said Richard Benjamin. "It's great to find rolling hills and then trees. When we left the highway we even discovered groves of fruit trees covering the hills."

Farther south, jagged rocks jut from the earth. The rugged sandstone cliffs of the Shawnee Hills form breathtaking canyons. This mountainous region, which extends from the Missouri Ozark Mountains, is called the Illinois Ozarks.

The view from the 300-million-year-old rocks overlooks sweeping dense forests. The surrounding Shawnee National Forest covers 268,400 acres of southern Illinois. Tupelo and cypress trees line the

MYSTERIOUS CAVES

Monroe County in southern Illinois has more than one hundred caves. They are carved out of limestone. Water on the surface of the rock seeps into the ground, picking up chemicals from the soil. The water becomes acid, like vinegar. It is so strong that it can eat into limestone, leaving cracks in the stone. Over many years, the cracks widen into large holes or caves.

Hidden inside are many unusual animals. Bats, salamanders, fish, and spiders live in the darkness. Birds and mammals stay near the mouths of the caves. Some larger caves, like Cave-in-Rock along the Ohio River, were once used as hideaways by pirates.

river swamps below. Here is where beavers, muskrats, and otters live.

In 1818, nearly one-fourth of Illinois was covered with wetland. Farming and mining claimed much of this land. Today, only 2.6 percent is swamp and bottomland forests. One hundred kinds of plants and animals live here, including the endangered prairie chicken.

The earliest pioneers in the Illinois Ozarks discovered natural salt and coal deposits beneath the Earth's surface. Once miners sapped these minerals, new settlers moved north. Now the region attracts mostly campers, birdwatchers, and fishermen.

TAMING THE WATERS

The greatest gift left by the glaciers were bodies of water. Illinois' network of waterways has helped turn the state into the nation's center of transportation. Long before settlers arrived, the Hopewell and Iliniwek traveled these waterways to trade with other native peoples. The first European pioneers cleared trees, planted grains, and mined along the Mississippi and Kaskaskia rivers. Today, cities and factories depend upon the state's lakes, rivers, and streams for drinking water, recreation, and shipping.

The Mississippi, the country's longest river, creates a natural border along western Illinois. The Ohio River runs down the state's southeast side. The Ohio and Mississippi come together in Cairo, at the state's southern tip.

Legend says the towns of Cairo and Thebes were named after the region's likeness to Egypt, whose Nile River enriches the soil along its banks. Northern counties had little rain one year in the early

1800s, and wheat fields dried up. But in southern counties rain fell and crops were plentiful. Author Russell Brownell wrote, "northerners came south seeking corn and wheat as to Egypt of old."

Lake Michigan connects northeastern Illinois with the other Great Lakes, which in turn are linked to the St. Lawrence River and the Atlantic Ocean. The lake's natural shoreline offered no harbors. Today's large harbors were dug at Chicago and Waukegan.

The Illinois River runs northeast through the state. One branch originally began about three miles short of the Chicago River, which

Cairo began as a trade center where the Ohio and Mississippi Rivers meet.

flowed into Lake Michigan. Native Americans carried canoes overland between the two waterways. In 1848, Illinoisans completed a canal joining branches of the two water routes, and a swampy fur trading settlement named Chicago burst into a major trading center. Chicago became the nation's only inland city to link a lake, river, and ocean.

Before 1887, the Chicago River, full of waste from outhouses and industry, flowed into the lake. Hundreds of Chicagoans died of diseases after drinking this filthy river water from the lake. So engineers decided to change the river's flow. They dug the south branch deeper, causing the water to pour into the ditch. The water changed its course and began to flow west and south away from Lake Michigan. From then on, the Chicago River was called the "river that flows backwards."

Illinois has another 282,000 acres of ponds and lakes and 430 rivers. The waterways teem with crappie, walleye, and perch. Bald cypress and sycamore trees line the beautiful banks. These state treasures offer endless fun for anyone who likes to canoe, camp, and fish.

The largest group of lakes is in Chain O'Lakes State Park, northwest of Chicago. Carlyle Lake in southern Illinois is the state's biggest manmade waterway. It covers 26,000 acres and runs along eighty-three miles of shoreline.

The strangest waterway is Rend Lake. Its **Y** shape came from damming the Big Muddy and Casey Fork rivers. The lake is along the Mississippi Flyway, the migration route for thousands of Canadian geese and ducks. American bald eagles live here year round.

"Off the beaten paths of the city," says journalist Bob Puhala,

"Awaiting discovery within these borders are fish-rich . . . reservoirs . . . lakes . . . and other south-flowing rivers," says TV outdoorsman Babe Winkelman.

"are rolling prairie views, high river bluffs, small-town paradises and backroad riches awaiting discovery."

SEASONS COME AND GO

"I don't like the weather here," admits a Chicago-born business-woman. "I'm not crazy about the hot summers and cold winters."

Many people dislike Illinois weather. Summers average 77 degrees Fahrenheit throughout the state. But the thermometer can

Charles Mound
(1,235 ft)

Galena

Rockford

Arlington
Hts.

Elgin

Batavia

Aurora

Naperville

Joliet

*Lake
Michigan*

Chicago

Hennepin Canal

Moline

Galesburg

Mississippi R.

Peoria

Illinois R.

Bloomington

Danville

Sangamon R.

Champaign

Quincy

Springfield

New Salem

Decatur

Kaskaskia R.

Effingham

Little Wabash R.

Wabash R.

*Carlyle
Lake*

East St.
Louis

Mt. Vernon

Mississippi R.

Carbondale

Ohio R.

LAND AND
WATER

reach much higher and for many days in a row further south. The highest recorded temperature was 117degrees in East St. Louis on July 14, 1954. In 1988, Illinoisans suffered forty-seven days of summer heat above 90 degrees.

Illinois air is very humid along its many waterways. From July 12 to July 16 in 1995, Chicago logged five brutal days of heat between 98 degrees and 104 degrees. High humidity made the heat feel worse. The city claimed over six hundred heat-related deaths during that time, more than any other midwestern state.

Winters are equally harsh. Temperatures can stay below freezing for weeks at a time. Illinois' average winter temperature is 30 degrees, but it drops lower further north. The coldest temperature on record is on January 22, 1930. On that day, Mount Carroll, a small town near the Wisconsin border, recorded a chilling –35 degrees.

In winter, fast-moving snowstorms can appear without warning. Chicago baseball fans know that spring and fall games can end abruptly due to unexpected snowstorms. Large cities stockpile salt for sudden snow and ice that can cripple traffic and bury whole neighborhoods.

Still, many Illinoisans prefer these extremes. "I like the four seasons," says senior citizen Gen Worshill. "I love autumn and spring. And winter holidays wouldn't be the same without snow."

Spring and summer breezes are delightful in Illinois. Yet gentle winds can pick up speed across the plains and bring wild shifts in weather any time of year. At times, moist air whips from the waterways. Early Chicagoans described Lake Michigan winds "as strong enough to strip the fur off a buffalo."

Thunderstorms and tornadoes pound cities and farms with

strong winds, sleet, and hail. Illinois averages twenty-six tornadoes each year. Many lose their force over the flatland or waterways. Others leave paths of death and destruction.

During July 1993, torrential rain fell over the Midwest. Rock Island reported 1.75 inches in twenty minutes, a huge amount. The endless rain caused massive flooding in most rivers, especially the Mississippi. About 30,000 people fled their homes and stores. More than 10,000 acres of farmland were soaked, costing billions of dollars in crops. Flooding renews the soil. But it also leaves rotted trees and abandoned homes and businesses, which can never be replaced.

The area around Prairie du Rocher, Illinois's oldest surviving town, was hit especially hard. Fifteen feet of water overflowed the two high stone levees along the Mississippi River, flooding the lowland farms leading into town. "Nobody had ever been through a natural disaster like that," agreed Debra and Jerry Burchell. "We rescued only a few goods from our shop at historic Fort de Chartres."

Still, local residents were heartened by the show of support during this crisis. About 6,500 National Guard arrived to remove residents and belongings. Volunteers rushed from throughout the state to help.

"My mom, younger brother, and I rode about three hours to a small town near Springfield," remembers fourteen-year-old Katie from Wilmette. "We shoveled sand into burlap bags. Other volunteers tied the bags and drove them in trucks to the river. People were really friendly." Together, Illinoisans can weather any storm—even horrendous floods and tornadoes.

2 ILLINOIS IN THE MAKING

"Kent Creek," by George Robertson

The earliest known people to call Illinois home hunted along the state's riverbanks ten thousand years ago. These Native Americans moved often to gather plants and track large animals for food. Many found shelter under limestone bluffs in what became southern Illinois.

Those who came after them stayed to build a new world. From about 1000 B.C. to A.D.1600 woodland Indians farmed squash, pumpkin, and other seed-bearing plants. They made pottery for cooking and storing food. They buried their dead in earth mounds. Future generations called them mound-builders.

MOUND-BUILDERS

Waves of mound-builders came over the next 1,100 years. The Hopewell established a network of trade routes from the Great Lakes to the Gulf of Mexico. Later Indians brought corn from Mexico. They invented bows and arrows and flint hoes for tilling the soil.

Major cities developed along the Mississippi River between A.D. 500 and 1500. The largest prehistoric site north of Mexico lies at Cahokia near present-day Collinsville. A chief and priests ruled from the top of massive platform mounds built in their honor. The people measured seasons, the time of day, and the stars with tall wooden poles. Archeologists named this sun calendar Woodhenge.

By 1150, Cahokia was one of the biggest cities in the world. Grass huts for about 20,000 people spread over nearly six square miles. Four thousand people crowded into each square mile, compared to 250 per square mile in most big cities today.

During the 1500s, the number of mound-builders slowly decreased. Some blame poor food, disease, or overcrowding for their disappearance. No one knows for sure. Visitors to the remaining mounds can only marvel and wonder.

THE ILINIWEK

The Iliniwek, meaning *the people*, were next to live in Illinois country. They planted cornfields and hunted buffalo. Their nation included the Cahokia, Peoria, Michigamea, Moingwena, and

The Hopewell honored their dead with a feast. They buried the dead in large mounds with shells, copper, and beads from their travels.

Father Marquette and Louis Jolliet traveled in birch bark canoes to the land of the Iliniwek.

Tamarou. These Algonquian-speaking tribes formed the largest family of Native Americans in the region.

In the early 1600s, warring Iroquois from the East invaded the Midwest Indians. They were searching for new fur-hunting grounds away from European settlers. The Iroquois forced the Sauk and Fox into Illinois, where the Rock and Mississippi rivers joined.

The first whites to explore Iliniwek country were French-Canadian Louis Jolliet and missionary Father Jacques Marquette. They reached the mouth of the Mississippi River on June 25, 1673.

Father Marquette wrote of a friendly meeting with the Indians:

"... in token of peace, they presented their pipes to smoke. They then invited us to their village where all the tribe awaited us . . ."

For the next ninety years, the French claimed the Illinois valley as theirs. They spelled Iliniwek as *Illinois*, and gave the name to the river where most Iliniwek lived. Later, Illinois became the state's name.

Accounts of peaceful Indians and good hunting attracted fur traders. Other priests came to convert the Indians to Christianity. They established their first permanent settlement near Cahokia.

Plentiful salt deposits that attracted animals and large buffalo herds brought whites to southern Illinois as well. Charles de St. Denis built a village and tannery near the Ohio River. His crew killed 13,000 buffalos for their hides and tongues. Local Indians murdered the tannery workers for their greed and waste. Few buffalo herds would roam southern Illinois ever again.

The French built three forts. Fort de Chartres and Fort Kaskaskia were government and military centers for the entire French-run Northwest Territory. Kaskaskia became a large village. Later, Fort de Chartres was rebuilt on its original foundation. Each year, neighbors gather in pioneer dress to remember the first French in Illinois country.

By the 1750s, the British demanded their share of the booming fur trade. They wanted control of all territory inland from their eastern colonies. French and British soldiers battled in what became known as the French and Indian War.

Indians joined the fight with France. They feared losing everything, as eastern Native Americans had, if the British invaded their land. But the French lost, and Kaskaskia fell to the British. In 1763,

France surrendered the entire Northwest Territory to the British. Many Indians moved west of the Mississippi River.

STATEHOOD

A series of treaties with Indians opened more of their land to settlers. Pioneers swarmed into Illinois and moved farther west. Steamboats revolutionized inland travel. Pioneers eyed Illinois country for its "soil 10 feet deep . . . fine as buckwheat flour . . . black as gunpowder." Groups of wooden shacks, farms, churches, and small towns appeared.

"Breaking Prairie," by Olof Krans. The first settlers planted food crops and flax. Oxen pulled the heavy plow through the soggy soil.

STATE FAIR

Where can you find a rodeo, carnival rides, pig races, funny-faced vegetables, and a huge cow carved in butter? At an Illinois state fair. Fairs are showcases for every form of agriculture and home-made product imaginable. In 1855, there was even a balloon. But the rope broke and two kids went for an overnight ride. After they landed safely, ballooning ended at fairs.

"Illinois' state fairs began in 1853 to bring farmers together," says fair historian Patricia Henry. "That way, isolated farmers could meet and benefit from learning and competing with each other."

Fairs were so popular that local counties created their own. But the state fair in Springfield is the king of fairs. Almost half a million people come to the 366-acre fairground. Every fair opens with a parade and ribbon-cutting ceremony by the governor. Then the fun begins!

New settlers pressed for joining the young United States. On December 3, 1818, Illinois became the twenty-first state and Kaskaskia its capital. With only 35,000 people, Illinois had the smallest population of any state admitted to the Union. Yet, it became the doorway to the nation's spirited westward frontier.

Most people clustered in southern Illinois and along the western river bottoms. To coax settlers northward, Congress awarded each soldier from the French and Indian War 160 acres of land between the Illinois and Mississippi rivers. By 1830 the state's population had grown to 150,000.

Blacksmith John Deere, however, had a better plan. Deere hated to stop every few feet to scrape the gloppy Illinois soil from his iron plow blades. While living in Grand Detour, he invented a steel plow blade that cut through the difficult soil. His invention revolutionized farming in Illinois country and brought settlers in even greater numbers to fill its soil.

The state capital moved two more times as new towns exploded with people. By 1839, lawmakers resettled in Springfield, where they stayed.

BLACK HAWK WAR

Pioneers drove many Indians into areas offering too little food. In 1832, Chief Black Hawk led 1,500 Sauk back into Illinois to regain their cornfields.

"My reason teaches me that land cannot be sold," wrote sixty-four-year-old Black Hawk. "The Great Spirit gave it to his children to live upon. So long as they occupy and cultivate it, they have a right to the soil."

Chief Black Hawk said of the Sauk defeat: "Black Hawk . . . cares about his people. They will suffer. He pities their fate."

Settlers disagreed. Fierce fighting broke out in what became the Black Hawk War. During four months of clashes, more than one thousand Indian men, women, and children died. In the end, Native Americans lost even more of their homeland. The Black Hawk War marked "the last Indian war fought east of the Mississippi River."

A LAND DIVIDED

From the beginning, the state divided deeply over the question of owning slaves. At statehood, four of every six Illinois residents came from the South. Unlike northerners, most southerners insisted they needed slaves to farm their fields. Many brought their ideas and their slaves with them into the northern state.

The Illinois constitution forbade slavery. Yet, the government allowed John Crenshaw to lease hundreds of slaves from owners in the slave state of Kentucky. Crenshaw's salt-making business prospered from the government-owned wells in Shawneetown, supplying 14 percent of Illinois' wealth from its profits. So state lawmakers let Crenshaw run his 30,000-acre estate as "a slave state within a free state." Terrible rumors spread through town about how Crenshaw kidnapped hundreds of free blacks and runaway slaves. People said he held them in chains on his mansion's third floor. Then he put them to work or sold them into slavery farther south.

During the 1830s and 1840s, many easterners and overseas immigrants flooded northern and central Illinois. The Illinois and Michigan Canal (I&M) opened the region to the Industrial Age. Newcomers built roads, mined coal, and manufactured goods. Many never understood how one person could own another. They pushed to end slavery in Illinois and throughout the nation.

Abraham Lincoln, a self-taught Springfield lawyer, tried to understand both sides. Finally, he reasoned that "although volume upon volume is written to prove slavery a very good thing, we never hear of the man who wishes to take the good of it by being a slave himself."

Groups for and against slavery organized around the state. Secret societies like the proslavery Knights of the Golden Circle plotted to help slaveowners. A mob killed Elijah Lovejoy of Alton for his writings to end slavery.

Women formed the Illinois AntiSlavery Society for Women. Free blacks worked with schools and churches to end local laws that favored catching runaway slaves. Illinois became an important path

Statesman Abraham Lincoln saved many remembrances of his youth. As a child he wrote:

"Abraham Lincoln his hand and pen. he will be good but god knows When."

Ransom Stowe, 33rd Illinois Infantry, was just fourteen years old when he enlisted in the Union Army.

along the Underground Railroad, the secret route to freedom for runaways.

In 1858, six-foot-four Abraham Lincoln ran against five-foot-four Stephen Douglas for United States Senator. Douglas, nicknamed "Little Giant," had championed running a railroad the length of the state. His plan linked southern businesses with the Great Lakes and caused many central Illinois towns to form around key railroad stops.

Lincoln and Douglas disagreed about slavery in a series of debates across Illinois. Lincoln argued that "American slavery and American liberty cannot co-exist on the same soil." He lost the election. But he gained national attention for Illinois and for himself as a great speaker against slavery. In 1860, Lincoln was elected the sixteenth president of the United States.

Soon after his election, the entire country erupted into Civil War. Some Knights of the Golden Circle pulled out their teeth rather than fight against slavery with the North. Soldiers needed teeth to bite on cartridges before loading their guns.

Many Illinoisans played a central role in the war. Almost 260,000 soldiers fought and about 35,000 died in battle. Galesburg's George Brown invented a new cornplanter machine that greatly increased the Midwest food supply to northern soldiers. Women formed aid societies to nurse sick soldiers and filled factory and professional jobs left by men who went to fight. Factory towns became major suppliers of weapons.

Moreover, Galena's General Ulysses S. Grant led troops to defeat General Robert E. Lee in the final battle of the war. After Lee surrendered, Grant told his troops, "The rebels are our Countrymen

A HERO PASSES

Author Carl Sandburg was struck by how much the people loved General Grant. After Grant died, seven-year-old Sandburg watched Galesburg citizens—black and white—honor their hero.

I remember a couple of cannon came past with six or eight horses pulling them. The Negro Silver Cornet Band marched. They were the only black faces in the parade, and as they passed I saw faces of men and women light up. . . there was something people liked about seeing the black men playing sad music because General Grant, who had helped them get free, was dead.

again." In 1868, Grant became the nation's eighteenth president, a post he held for two terms.

The person most credited with keeping the country together and ending slavery was Abraham Lincoln. Five days after the war officially ended, however, Lincoln was shot. A grieving nation buried him in a tomb in Springfield. In central Illinois places that marked every step of his remarkable career became historic sites. Today, Illinoisans proudly call their state "the Land of Lincoln."

"CHICAGO SHALL RISE AGAIN"

Illinois thrived after the Civil War. State farmers raised the most corn and wheat in the nation. More railroad miles than any other state linked farm towns with cities where crops were sold. Hogs and cows became big business in Illinois, especially in Chicago stockyards. Illinois had become the nation's breadbasket.

Then, on October 8, 1871, Chicago almost died. At about 9:00 P.M., fire erupted in Kate and Patrick O'Leary's barn. Legend blames a cow for kicking over the lantern. But the exact cause of the fire remains unknown.

What followed were twenty-seven hours of terror. Thirty-mile-an-hour winds spread flames wildly toward the city's center. Tinderbox wooden houses and stores fell like dominos. Soon the extreme heat and sparks jumped the Chicago River. The fire raged out of control.

One observer wrote: "There was sudden screaming and dashing about of half-clad women, gathering up valuables . . . frantic rushing into the streets . . . Everywhere dust, smoke, flame, heat, thunder of falling walls, crackle of fire, hissing of water, panting of engine, roar of wind, and uproar."

A light rain helped cool the last ashes. By then, nearly 20,000 buildings lay in ruin. About 300 people had died, and 104,500 were homeless.

Chicago was rebuilt with amazing speed. New fire codes required steel and stone buildings that resisted fire. *Chicago Daily* headlines declared, "Chicago Shall Rise Again."

Chicago healed in time to hold the 1893 World's Columbian Exposition. The city put on a grand show for the fair. Magnificent buildings, the first Observation wheel, and art from around the world showcased the city and state.

Factories sprang up throughout Illinois. By 1900, Illinois had fourteen cities with more than 100,000 people. Chicago was the state's largest city, with almost 1.7 million people. Waves of Euro-

Away from the downtown blaze, newsboys called for buyers to read about the great Chicago Fire.

pean immigrants and southern blacks flooded in to work in food-processing plants, clothing factories, steel mills, and construction.

Wealthy business owners prospered in Chicago. But their workers suffered greatly. Most toiled ten- to fourteen-hour workdays in filthy, unsafe conditions. At night, they went home to overcrowded, rundown neighborhoods.

Many major labor protests began in Chicago. Workers organized

EL-A-NOY

The unknown poet who wrote the flowery words to "El-a-noy" was inspired by the Biblical King Solomon and the Queen of Sheba, as well as by the twelfth-century French philosopher Peter Abelard and the great love of his life, the fair Heloise.

Way down—up-on the Wa-bash, Such land was nev-er known. If Ad-am had passed o-ver it, The soil he'd sure-ly own. He'd think it was the gar-den he'd played in when a boy, And straight pro-nounce it E-den in the State of El-a noy.

Then move your fam-'ly west-ward, Good health you will en-joy, And rise to wealth and hon-or in the State of El - a - noy.

'Twas here the Queen of Sheba came,
With Solomon of old,
With an ass-load of spices,
Pomegranates and fine gold;
And when she saw this lovely land,
Her heart was filled with joy,
Straightway she said: "I'd like to be
A Queen in El-a-noy." *Chorus*

She's bounded by the Wabash,
The Ohio and the Lakes,
She's crawfish in the swampy lands,
The milk-sick and the shakes;
But these are slight diversions
And take not from the joy
Of living in this garden land,
The State of El-a-noy. *Chorus*

Away up in the northward,
Right on the border line,
A great commercial city,
Chicago, you will find.
Her men are all like Abelard,
Her women like Heloise;
All honest virtuous people,
For they live in El-a-noy. *Chorus*

to call for eight-hour workdays, increased wages, and laws against children working. Chicagoan Mary O'Reilly explains the struggle:

> Just to labor for bread,
> Just to work and be fed.
> For this we have marched
> Through the snow-covered street.

On May 4, 1886, a bomb exploded at a peaceful Chicago worker rally in Haymarket Square. Police panicked, and violence exploded. After a flurry of gunfire, seven policemen and two onlookers lay dead.

The police arrested eight labor leaders for causing the riot. After an unfair trial, four were hung, and one committed suicide. Later, the governor cleared the others.

A statue in front of the police department training center honors the policemen who died. At first, Chicago workers observed special May Day celebrations to remember their dead friends. Then the idea of honoring workers spread around the world. Today, the day that began as a remembrance of Chicagoans is celebrated in eastern Europe and Russia as well.

Jane Addams of Cedarville started the settlement house movement in the United States to ease problems of the poor. She opened Hull House in Chicago as a safe place within a slum. From here, Addams fought for better jobs, schools, housing, garbage collection, and health care. Her fight spurred the nation into giving poor people ways to improve their lives.

Even with its troubles, Illinois led the country on many issues. In 1891, the state was first to pass child labor laws and create separate

Hull House classes served immigrant families who worked at the nearby stock-yards and lived in crowded slums. Irish, German, Russian, Italian, Jewish, and Polish immigrants found friends and shelter here.

courts for children. Illinois provided wages to sick workers and passed the first "mother's aid" law, granting money for the care of helpless children.

The boldest move, however, came in 1913. Illinois was the first state east of the Mississippi River to allow women to vote. Strong women like Jane Addams and Myra Bradwell, the state's first woman lawyer, pushed for women's rights at home and in the workplace. Bradwell fought so Illinois women could keep their own

POPULATION GROWTH: 1810–1990

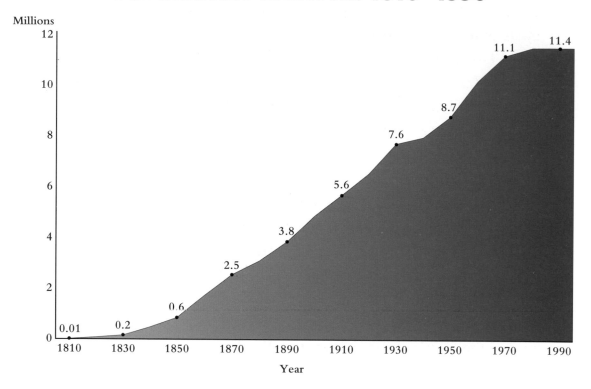

Millions

12

10

8

6

4

2

0

11.4

11.1

8.7

7.6

5.6

3.8

2.5

0.6

0.2

0.01

1810 1830 1850 1870 1890 1910 1930 1950 1970 1990

Year

wages and care for their children after divorce. Many women claim that Bradwell "probably changed the course of women's legal rights."

ILLINOIS TODAY

Illinois continued to lead the country in farming, industry, and transportation into the twentieth century. The state played a major role during World Wars I and II. City factories in Chicago, Rockford, Peoria, and Rantoul worked overtime to make weapons, tanks, and planes. National weapons storehouses developed in Joliet and Rantoul. Once again, farmers shipped foods to wartorn areas to feed the soldiers.

On December 2, 1942, University of Chicago's Enrico Fermi and a team of scientists discharged the first nuclear chain reaction. This experiment led to the first atomic bomb, which helped end World War II. Moreover, Fermi's discovery ushered our nation and the world into the atomic age.

The country's postwar boom swept Illinois along with it. Factories turned to making profitable peacetime goods. Argonne National Laboratory near Chicago opened an atomic research center. Fermi Laboratory in Batavia created the world's most powerful atom smasher. By 1960, Chicago was the country's largest steel producer and a leader in computer and atomic energy research.

But population and business changes that troubled the nation during the 1970s and 1980s eventually affected Illinois. Interstate highways cut through farms. Motels and shopping malls opened near exits. Shoppers drove to the outskirts of town, leaving city centers to decay.

Prices for farm products dropped, causing profits to decline. Many farmers sold their land and went into higher paying work. City factories moved to suburbs or other states. Others produced goods overseas where costs were cheaper.

Without industry taxes to pay for services, cities and towns suffered. Poor schools, increased crime, and run-down housing ruined many neighborhoods. People with money moved to the suburbs or followed jobs out of the state.

Others gave up on big-city life and left for smaller towns.

Debbie Brooks left a good chemist's job to live in Chester, an Illinois town of about eight thousand people. "I like little towns like this," she said. "The quality of life is better, and there's less crime than in a big city."

Towns like Chester are the future of Illinois. They attract people from big cities everywhere. Chicago will continue to thrive. But Illinoisans work hard to balance the growth of every region, from teeming cities to small farm communities.

The old water tower, the only building to survive the Chicago Fire, stands tall among the city's newer skyscrapers.

3 POWER, JOBS, AND MONEY

The Capitol in Springfield

"**I**llinois has many strengths," says State Representative Jeffrey Schoenberg. "We just need to coordinate between the city of Chicago and the rest of the state."

INSIDE GOVERNMENT

Illinois government tries to balance the interests of all its citizens. Nearly five thousand workers carry out jobs for one of three government branches: executive, legislative, judicial.

Executive. Every four years, Illinois voters elect six officers for the executive branch. The governor serves as head of all executive departments and committees, just as the U.S. president does. Each governor prepares a yearly state budget, appoints hundreds of managers, approves or vetoes (rejects) bills and contracts, and oversees the state military.

Legislative. The Illinois legislature, called the General Assembly, includes 59 senators and 118 representatives. Voters select one representative from each district every two years. Senators serve for four years.

The General Assembly creates or changes laws and approves the state budget. A majority of members in each house votes to pass a bill. Then the governor signs it into law. If the governor vetoes the bill, three-fifths of the assembly can still vote it into law.

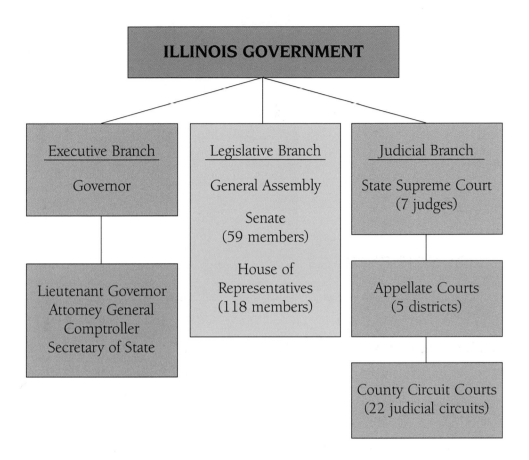

ILLINOIS GOVERNMENT

Executive Branch

Governor

Lieutenant Governor
Attorney General
Comptroller
Secretary of State

Legislative Branch

General Assembly

Senate
(59 members)

House of
Representatives
(118 members)

Judicial Branch

State Supreme Court
(7 judges)

Appellate Courts
(5 districts)

County Circuit Courts
(22 judicial circuits)

Judicial. The judicial branch of government includes more than 400 elected judges and the 350 associate judges they appoint. Their job is to translate the state constitution into law.

Most citizens appear before one of twenty-two county circuit courts. Those unhappy with a ruling can appear before an Appellate Court or the highest state Supreme Court. Cook County's Circuit Court, which includes Chicago, has the most judges in the nation. Even with 177 judges, people often wait months for their hearing.

Mayor Richard J. Daley demanded that his workers follow orders. One alderman said, "It's one-man rule. You're dead if he doesn't like you."

THE CHICAGO MACHINE AND DOWNSTATE

Illinois divides into more bodies of local government than any other state. This confusing assortment of government agencies often overlap and compete for money and power. Some of the state's biggest struggles are between Chicago and the rest of the state.

Chicago's mayor Richard J. Daley built a powerful city "machine" between 1955 and 1976. His idea of government was to trade favors, such as jobs, for votes. Poor people even received terrible threats. "Don't vote [my way] and you lose your public housing or food checks."

Daley's Chicago became known as "the city that worked." Moreover, Daley produced an empire that reached into state government and national elections. Illinois earned the reputation as the Midwest president-maker because Daley could guarantee votes to national candidates. "What Daley needs, Daley gets," said one observer.

Daley's machine created great distrust among Illinois districts, which continues to this day. Those outside the city believe Chicago politicians hold too much power. Chicago, with half the state's population, pushes big-city programs such as enlarging airports. Growing suburbs want their own needs met, such as expanding highways to meet increased traffic demands.

"Downstaters feel their concerns are better heard by a downstater as governor," admits Rantoul mayor, Katy Podagrosi.

ILLINOIS AND THE NATION

Illinois voters also send two senators and twenty representatives to represent them in federal government. Of these, 23 percent are women. "Illinois can take pride in the fact that it sent the first African American and woman to the Senate, Carol Mosely-Braun," says Janice Cooper, director of a Washington watchdog group.

Ideally, government bodies at every level work together. Joint programs bring extra money, power, and staff to solve local problems. For example, Illinois had the fourth highest violent crime rating of any state in 1994. Shock waves shot through state and federal government. United States senators Mosely-Braun and Paul Simon launched federal appeals against television violence and for gun control. Governor Jim Edgar signed the 1995 Violence Prevention Act, a new state public safety program.

Newly elected U.S. Senator Carol Mosely-Braun gives her son a victory hug. She was the first woman and first black ever to hold a major office in Cook County government. Coworkers in the Illinois House of Representatives voted her best legislator for ten years.

Local villages, like Wilmette, banned gun ownership. State Representative Schoenberg beat back the state's ten thousand licensed gun dealers, who wanted to overturn local gun control laws. These joint efforts were only the beginning of a long fight to make Illinois streets safe.

LAWS FOR KIDS

Illinois has many laws to protect kids. Stores cannot sell liquor to anyone under eighteen years. Only children sixteen or over can work, unless they are part of a special program. Even then, laws limit the number of hours and type of work. Newer state laws punish divorced parents who refuse to pay for raising their children. Safehouses and child abuse and runaway hotlines help kids in trouble.

Illinois laws grant kids certain rights. Kids can vote at eighteen years old. They can take driver's education at age fifteen and apply for a driver's license at age sixteen. In return, they must be good citizens by following its laws. Illinois kids stay in school between ages seven and sixteen, pass a Constitution test in eighth grade, and use seat belts when riding in cars.

Illinois sponsors several programs to help kids protect themselves. Project DARE (Drug Abuse Resistance Education) is the state's most sweeping youth program, reaching about one million students statewide. The Illinois Police Department trains officers to help kids resist drugs, gangs, violence, and the problems they cause. Illinois wants kids prepared to make the best choices for their lives.

ILLINOISANS AT WORK

"Since the 1960s, we went from a sleepy rural town to regional trade center of 15,000 but serving 90,000 people," claims Marion's Chamber of Commerce director. "We have a diverse economy of government services and industry plus the perfect location along the highway for travel."

Teenagers hang out in their Chicago neighborhood.

Illinois' main strength is its varied economy. The state thrives, even with pockets of high unemployment. The flow of industry leaving the state in the 1980s has slowed.

Illinois still plays a major role in agriculture, manufacturing, mining, and, of course, transportation. But Illinois workers have adapted to service industries, which are taking over the U.S. economy.

Service Industries. Anyone who helps other workers perform their duties holds a service job. Illinois has a record number of jobs in government programs, hospitals, law and insurance companies, banks and media. Service workers account for three-fourths of the jobs in Illinois.

And that includes kids, too. Charles Hays created the School Safety Patrol in 1920 when he was president of Chicago-based AAA Motor Club. Since then, millions of children have served as crossing guards. Patrol boys and girls are credited with saving countless lives by helping other kids cross streets on their way to school.

With half the state's population, Chicago has the greatest number of service jobs. More health and medical associations keep their headquarters here. The city claims the nation's largest printer, R.R. Donnelly, and oldest mail order house, Montgomery Ward, which runs several department stores today.

Even with city businesses closing or moving, Chicago remains the financial capital of the Midwest. Four major Chicago financial institutions, including the Midwest Stock Exchange, monitor our nation's businesses. And buyers and sellers trade more goods at the Chicago Board of Trade than anywhere else in the world.

Tourism in Illinois is a growing service business. The state opened visitor centers throughout the state and is online with computers to help travelers locate the best stops. Visitors spend over $15 billion each year in Illinois, making it one of the ten most traveled states.

Chicago draws the largest share of tourists and business travelers. Chicago's O'Hare Airport is the busiest airport in the world, handling more than 160,000 passengers each day. Still, smaller towns praise local heros, honor their natural historic sites, and trumpet home-grown products as a way to attract visitors to the most hidden areas of the state.

Fertile Fields and Productive Mines. Just three percent of Illinois workers are farmers. Yet Illinois is among the top five agriculture states nationwide. It sends more farm products overseas than any state except Iowa.

Illinoisans are the country's leading soybean growers. Only Iowa rivals Illinois for the nation's most corn. Northern Illinois provides hogs, the state's chief meat animal, Swiss cheese, and seeds and

Illinois ranks second among the states in raising and marketing hogs.

PUMPKIN DELIGHTS

Toasted Pumpkin Seeds

Illinois is the number one pumpkin-growing state, and Sycamore has the "World's Greatest Pumpkin Festival." But Native Americans grew pumpkins and roasted the seed hundreds of years ago. You can, too.

Just scoop the seeds from inside the pumpkin and wash them. Spread the seeds on a greased cookie sheet. Shake salt lightly over the seeds.

Ask an adult to set the oven to about 200°F. Then toast the seeds in the oven for about thirty minutes, until they look dry. Let the seeds cool for a while. Then try not to eat them all at once.

Snack Bars

Making *pumpkin snack bars* is one way the townspeople of Sycamore prepare their pumpkins today.

1. Preheat the oven to 350°F. (Ask an adult for help.)
2. Mix 1 package of spice cake mix (2-layer), 1 can of pumpkin (16 oz.), three-quarters cup sweet mayonnaise salad dressing, and 3 eggs in a mixing bowl.
3. Pour the mixture into a greased 15x10x1-inch baking pan.
4. Bake about 20 minutes or until a toothpick comes out dry from the center.
5. Frost with your favorite prepared frosting. Slice the cake into bars and enjoy.

BROOM CORN BROOMS

Did you know that Illinois was once the broom corn capital of the world? Fields of broom corn, which looks like sorghum cane, covered central Illinois. A major broom producing industry grew up around the town of Arcola.

"The problem was broom corn needed about 300 people to harvest," remembers Alvin Wingler, president of Warren Broom Company. "Farmers could make more money growing corn."

Many of the nation's brooms are still handmade in Arcola. Mexican yucca plant fibers have replaced most Midwest broom corn. But Arcola still celebrates its role in making brooms with an annual Broom Corn Festival.

bulbs, especially gladioli. Cobden peaches, Murphysboro apples, and Sycamore pumpkins give these towns reasons to show off their popular local products with yearly festivals.

Illinois is blessed with the nation's greatest variety of underground resources. The state produces the most fluorite in the world. Fluorite, which is used in steel, glass, and chemicals, is the state's second major mineral.

Illinois has a surprising amount of oil. Most oil wells are in the southeast. Still, oil supplies less than 2 percent of the state's energy. Nuclear power furnishes 55 percent of the electric power. The rest comes from coal, the state's mineral treasure.

Coal lies below two-thirds of the state, providing much of Illinois' mining wealth. Galena once produced 85 percent of the nation's lead. Today, some lead and zinc mines remain in Galena. But six percent of the nation's coal comes from mines in southern Illinois. The most famous coal mine of all, however, is in the Museum of Science and Industry in Chicago—for everyone to visit.

Farm Tools, Foods, and Steel Mills. One in five Illinois jobs come from manufacturing. Illinois factories produce equipment that is exported around the world. Farm and construction machinery account for the largest share.

John Deere started his tractor company in Grand Detour more than 150 years ago. Now it is an international corporation headquartered in Moline. Caterpillar in Peoria ranks among the world's major manufacturers of construction equipment, with divisions overseas. Other large equipment and car factories developed in Peoria, Normal, and Belvidere.

Illinois is a leading food processing state. Many companies that

Powerful machines called combines harvest and unload corn into large bins.

pioneered chewing gum, hot dogs, and candy bars began in the Chicago area. Today, candy, meat, and dairy products are prepared in factories statewide along with household goods and parts for telephones, computers, and cars.

A CHANGING ECONOMY

Since the 1970s, many large factories have closed, moved, or cut staff. Changes in factory methods and cheaper labor and raw

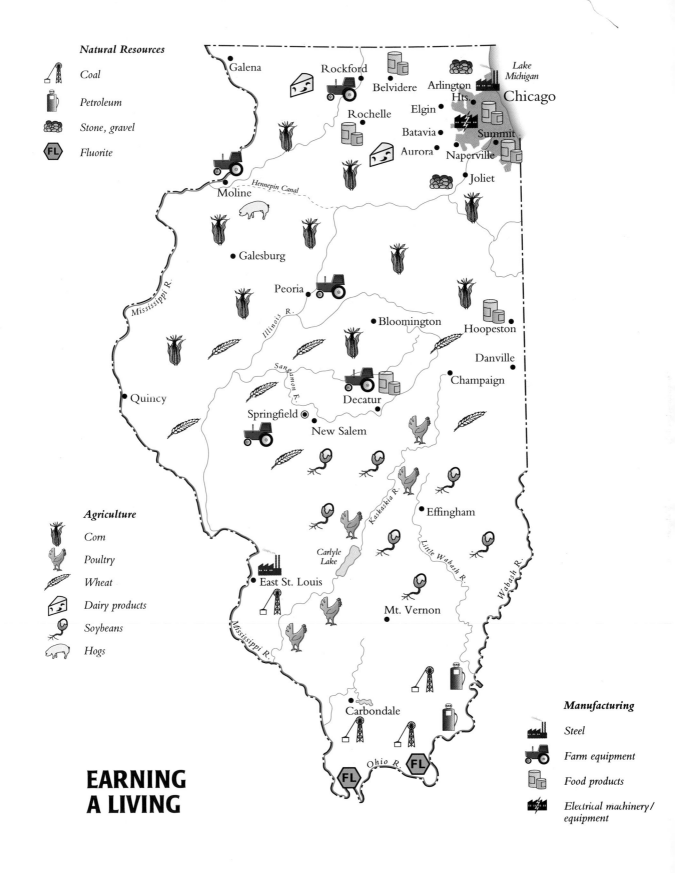

Natural Resources

Coal

Petroleum

Stone, gravel

FL Fluorite

Agriculture

Corn

Poultry

Wheat

Dairy products

Soybeans

Hogs

Manufacturing

Steel

Farm equipment

Food products

Electrical machinery/ equipment

Galena

Rockford

Belvidere

Arlington Hts.

Elgin

Lake Michigan

Chicago

Rochelle

Batavia

Aurora

Naperville

Summit

Joliet

Hennepin Canal

Moline

Galesburg

Peoria

Illinois R.

Bloomington

Hoopeston

Danville

Mississippi R.

Sangamon R.

Decatur

Champaign

Quincy

Springfield

New Salem

Kaskaskia R.

Effingham

Little Wabash R.

Wabash R.

Carlyle Lake

East St. Louis

Mississippi R.

Mt. Vernon

Carbondale

Ohio R.

FL

FL

EARNING A LIVING

materials elsewhere meant some older factories could not keep up. Factory closings can be a terrible blow to communities.

During the 1980s, steel mills outside Chicago shut down. The air around the mills cleared without smokestacks spitting out smelly gases. But the loss of mills cost many jobs. Without wages to buy goods, stores closed and people moved. Nearby neighborhoods decayed.

"Ma and pa businesses struggled," said one Hegewisch resident. "People traveled downtown for jobs or went into service industries as police and firefighters."

Today, local leaders are still working to tear down abandoned

1992 GROSS STATE PRODUCT: $295 BILLION

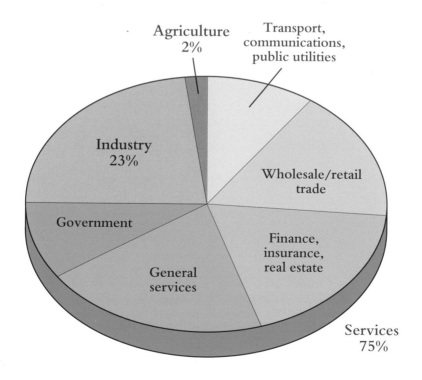

steel mills. They hope to develop the land into other businesses. Then jobs will return to south Chicago.

Similar challenges hit service jobs after the federal government closed several military bases, including Rantoul's 76-year-old Air Force Base. Rantoul's population of 17,000 dropped by 5,000 people. Townspeople who worked at the base lost their jobs. And Rantoul was left with thousands of acres of unused land.

"We had more problems than if a factory closed," remembers Mayor Katy Podagrosi. "The base had a hospital, water system, electricity, airport, and 1,400 houses. We acquired a full city within a city."

Over the next five years, kids said goodbye to long-time friends. The school's ethnic population changed. At home, many children worried about parents who had lost their jobs.

City and federal planners acted quickly to design a new community. By 1995, Rantoul attracted more than 2,500 jobs for seven major companies housed on the base. Social services, education and recreation, and business offices filled the buildings. Hangar Four became an Aerospace Museum, complete with combat jets and a missile silo.

"Rantoul feels good about itself," Podagrosi says. "The country feels good about us, too."

Illinois lawmakers seek new business throughout the state. They participate in yearly fairs in Mexico City to promote Illinois industries in Latin America. Government and business leaders visit companies overseas regularly. They want foreign companies to open factories in the state and buy Illinois products. People from Illinois are survivors.

PROTECTING THE ENVIRONMENT

Illinois has a terrible record concerning the environment. Factories, businesses, and heavily populated cities take a great toll on natural resources. In addition, Illinois allots less money than most states for protecting its resources.

In 1995, the state introduced a program to raise money for state parks. Car and truck owners can choose special license plates with the colorful state bird, the cardinal, and the state prairie grass, big bluestem. These plates cost more. But the extra money goes to improve parks and hire park workers.

Problems with the Illinois environment go beyond money, however. Every person in Illinois produces more than a ton of garbage a year. Waste seeps into the air and water, changing the environment for plants and animals.

Illinois is running out of places to put its waste. Towns battle over where to bury garbage. Once the state was mostly flatland. Now more than 117 landfills have formed grassed-over mountains of garbage everywhere.

In 1990, state lawmakers adopted a series of laws to limit harmful waste. Grass clippings and leaves are no longer burned. Instead, they are left on the lawn, saved for compost, or hauled away for giant compost piles.

Many local districts run strict programs to reuse and recycle waste. Homeowners and businesses separate plastic, paper, glass, and metal containers for garbage pickups. Then the materials are taken to recycling centers.

Other laws addressed problems of factory waste spoiling air and water. Counties with recreation areas restricted hunting and fishing. Major efforts went into listing and saving endangered plants and animals.

In Chicago, rows of trees planted along busy highways absorb car gases. City planners cleaned the muddy Chicago River. The giant Deep Tunnel project improved sewerage treatment, making the river a pleasant "second lakefront." Greenery grew so thick that deer returned to the river's North Branch.

Illinois lawmakers believe that kids hold the key to protecting the environment. The state trains teachers to help kids enjoy and save nature. The Department of Conservation holds Arbor Day contests and publishes fun nature-related materials. Illinois wants kids involved in the future of their state.

These girls are working on a community garden project sponsored by the nonprofit home building group, Habitat for Humanity.

4 EVERYDAY ILLINOISANS

Celebrating Kwanza

"It's bad luck to step over a broom," warns Abe Lincoln's Irish-English father. "An itchy nose means you'll kiss a fool," reminds a Russian-Jewish grandmother. "If you toss your shoe in the air and it lands standing up, you will have good luck that day," explains a Wilmette woman born in Tokyo, Japan.

Unusual sayings color almost everyone's childhood in Illinois. With the sayings come varied customs, religions, and foods. Many of these customs are brought by recent immigrants to Illinois. Others have been passed down through families that have lived in the state for many generations.

POPULATIONS THROUGHOUT THE STATE

With 11.4 million people in 1990, Illinois has the sixth largest population in the United States. Eighty-five percent of these people live in cities, mostly in Chicago. Crowded city neighborhoods mean more people compete for houses and jobs. The rest of Illinoisans live in the country, mostly on farms.

Cities and towns celebrate their ethnic roots. Many were named by their original settlers. Moline, meaning "milltown" in French, has one of the largest Belgian communities outside Belgium. In

TEN LARGEST CITIES

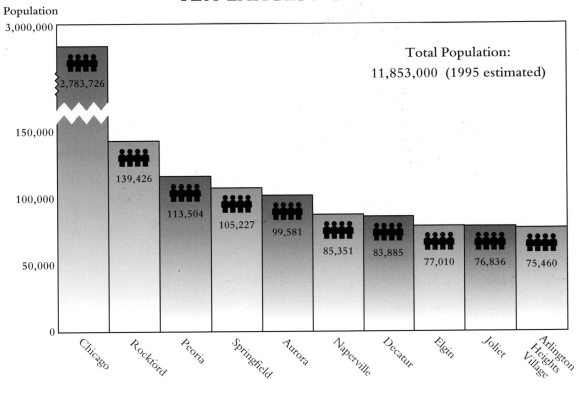

Population

Total Population:
11,853,000 (1995 estimated)

3,000,000

2,783,726

150,000

139,426

100,000

113,504

105,227

99,581

85,351

83,885

77,010

76,836

75,460

50,000

0

Chicago · Rockford · Peoria · Springfield · Aurora · Naperville · Decatur · Elgin · Joliet · Arlington Heights Village

1907, the city claimed the first newspaper in the United States written in Flemish. Today, Moline is a melting pot of Belgians, Greeks, African Americans, and Mexican Americans.

Illinois attracts greater numbers of recent immigrants than any Midwest state. Changes in Latin America and overseas in the Middle East and Eastern Europe spur some immigrants to seek a better life here. The number of Latin Americans and Asians is especially on the rise.

Most Illinois immigrants come to Chicago for the variety of jobs. Networks of churches and synagogues work with refugee groups

Members of a Latino Little League baseball team in Chicago keep their eyes on the game.

to bring people from countries where they are in danger. Chicago alone has more than 50,000 Guatemalans.

Chicago has the greatest ethnic diversity of any American city outside of New York City and Washington, D.C. Mexicans total nearly 30 percent of the city's foreign born. Another 10 percent come from Poland to form the largest Polish community outside Poland. And there is a large Japanese-American community. Many moved from California after the outbreak of World War II.

Newcomers represent nearly every country of the world. Restaurants offer everything from pad thai and sweet Thai noodles to homemade tortillas. Students in one northside Chicago school speak thirty-five different languages, including Urdu, Mayan, and Vietnamese. The test is to find teachers who can talk to children in their native language while helping them adjust to America.

"Here kids are taught fifty-fifty in their language and English in our school. After three years, they are thrown to the wolves, totally in English-speaking classes," says teacher Lucy Klocksin.

So many Indian-owned stores line west Devon Avenue that the area is called Sari Capital of the Midwest. Indian women travel hundreds of miles to buy material for their loose-fitting clothes. One stretch of the street has been renamed Gandhi Boulevard after the famous Indian peaceseeker.

The next mile is Golda Meir boulevard. This section honors the

ETHNIC ILLINOIS

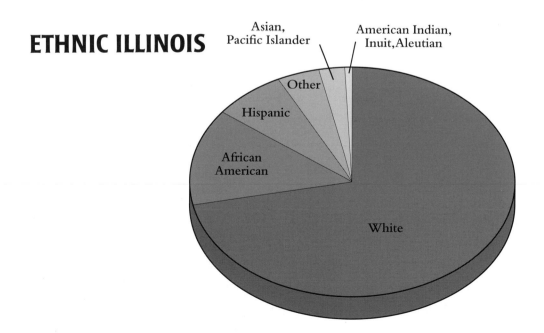

Russian-born American who became Israel's beloved prime minister from 1969 to 1974. Her name on street signs reflects the neighborhood's Israeli and strict Jewish populations.

BLACK COMMUNITIES

About 15 percent of Illinoisans and 40 percent of Chicagoans are African American. This group, more than others, has faced many racial barriers. Yet, African Americans have played an important role in the state's progress.

Haitian-born Jean Baptiste Point du Sable was Illinois' first non-Native American permanent settler about 1779. He and his wife Catherine, a Potawatomi, built a thriving trade center on what is now Chicago's elegant Michigan Avenue. Twenty years later, he moved his family to East Peoria with the Potawatomi.

Runaway slaves trickled into Illinois during the early 1800s and settled near Underground Railroad stations. After the Civil War in 1865, larger numbers of freed blacks came. Most settled along major railway routes, forming communities in Jacksonville, Champaign, Galesburg, and Chicago.

George W. Smith, an escaped slave, was one of the first successful black landowners in Illinois. He saved to buy eighty acres of land in 1876. By 1900, he owned 437 acres in Champaign county. His youngest son, John Smith, expanded the farm to 600 acres. John died in 1968. The family has kept the farm as a memorial to their ancestors who struggled so hard to succeed. World Wars I and II triggered large black migrations northward to fill wartime jobs and find greater freedom. Busloads of blacks left poor farms in

Kentucky for the northern "promised land." Crossing the border into Cairo, Illinois, caused the greatest thrill.

According to the *Tribune,* "There black passengers did something they never would have dreamed of doing in the south. They moved to seats at the front of the bus." In Kentucky, they would have been jailed or beaten for sitting there.

By 1918, 60,000 blacks lived in Chicago alone. Poet Carl Sandburg reported, "Every time a lynching takes place in a

Jean Baptiste Point du Sable founded Chicago as a trading settlement with a large main building, two barns, a mill, bake house, poultry house, workshop, dairy, and smokehouse. He employed many French and Native American workers.

Elizabeth (Bessie) Coleman earned the first international pilot's license granted to an American by a French aviation school. She became famous in the United States for parachuting and stunt flying.

community down south . . . people from that community will arrive in Chicago inside of two weeks."

Many reached fame never dreamed of in the south. Adelbert Roberts became the first black state senator in 1924. Bessie Coleman was the first woman and black to earn a pilot's license. The highway leading to Chicago's O'Hare Airport honors her triumphs.

Yet African Americans never really escaped racial hatred in the north. Unwritten laws limited most blacks to cramped neighborhoods and low-paying jobs as railroad porters, maids, and day workers. Angry city blacks pushed for better jobs, schools, and housing and for an end to police cruelty. Widespread tensions between whites and African Americans erupted in 1917. A white mob swept through East St. Louis, burning 240 black-owned buildings and killing fifty people. Within two years, the madness spread to Chicago.

Rock-throwing whites killed a black boy who swam past an imaginary line separating the black group's beaches from the ones used by whites. Violence exploded after police refused to arrest the killers. Three days of rage left twenty blacks and fourteen whites dead, more than one hundred injured, and scores of black homes burned.

Chicago's black population rose from 492,000 to 1 million between 1950 and 1970. The south side became known as the black capital of America. Black culture flowered as world-famous musicians, writers, and artists got their start here.

In 1968, riots erupted once again. After Reverend Martin Luther King, Jr., the famous African-American civil rights leader, was shot, Chicago blacks ripped through streets, burning entire neighborhoods. During the 1980s, fires smoldered. Poor blacks felt abandoned by state and federal governments. Severe budget cuts limited programs for better jobs, schools, and homes. Many hopeless youth turned to drugs and the violence it brings.

Today, violence in some neighborhoods is so widespread that kids fear walking to school or playgrounds. Parents in Chicago housing projects worry their kids won't live until another birthday. One mother pays $80 a month for burial insurance for her five children, who are under thirteen years of age.

However, a generation of successful blacks have come from years

Some Chicago housing projects were so run-down the city began to wreck the buildings in 1995.

In 1989, Oprah Winfrey was chosen as Ms Magazine's "Woman of the Year" for her successful television talk show. The magazine said Winfrey "showed women they can climb as high as they want."

of racial conflict in Illinois. Many are celebrated artists, such as blues singer Muddy Waters, and sports figures, including basketball superstar Michael Jordan, as well as United States Senator Carol Mosely-Braun and John Harold Johnson, a leading Chicago businessman. One of the most well-known African Americans is Oprah Winfrey. She is a respected actress, talk-show host, owner of Harpo Studios, and the third richest person in the United States.

RELIGIONS

Illinoisans practice a range of religions that mirror their varied origins. More people throughout the state follow Christian religions, mainly Roman Catholic and Protestant sects of Presbyterian, Baptist, Methodist, and Lutheran. Larger cities support Jewish synagogues, Greek Orthodox churches, Buddhist shrines, and Muslim mosques.

Wilmette is home to the awesome Bahai House of Worship. The Bahai religion was founded in Persia, now Iran, more than one hundred years ago. The Bahais chose Wilmette as the center of their North American movement. Wilmette's grand lacy-domed building took forty years to complete. The white marble palace is one of only seven Bahai houses of worship worldwide.

The long-standing "peace" churches of Mennonites, Mormons, and Society of Friends have large followings in Illinois. In 1839, Mormon prophet Joseph Smith led followers to Nauvoo, meaning "beautiful place" in Hebrew. He founded the town after religious abuse forced the Mormons out of Missouri. Nauvoo prospered so much other settlers feared Mormon power. They killed Smith and his brother and chased most Mormons to Utah.

Future French and German settlers kept old Nauvoo. Today, the Reorganized Church of Latter-day Saints operates a visitor site that preserves the Mormon shrine. Each August, Mormons present the outdoor musical, "City of Joseph." The people of Nauvoo hold ceremonies on Labor Day to remember the waves of immigrants that farmed grapes and churned cheese, as their European ancestors did.

For some communities, church activities guide every aspect of

WEDDING OF THE WINE AND CHEESE

Long ago in southern France, a shepherd boy forgot his lunch in a cave. Curds, the thick part of cheese, and bread sat in the cool limestone cave for many months. When he returned, the boy discovered that the bread totally spoiled. But surprisingly the curds were protected by tasty blue streaks of mold. The French who came to Nauvoo claim this was the beginning of blue cheese.

Nauvoo celebrates an Annual Grape Festival the weekend before Labor Day. At the festival, actors stage a wedding between the bride of wine and bridegroom of cheese. The marriage symbolizes how well this food and drink go together. A shepherd boy appears in the ceremony, leading the way to the perfect marriage of tastes.

Enclosed horse-drawn buggies stand outside Amish farms, where everything the family needs is made by hand.

economic and social life. Amish live the same simple lifestyle as when they were driven from Switzerland during the mid-1800s. Work and prayer fill their days.

The Amish reject such trappings of the modern world as electricity, cars, and television. Instead, they travel by horse-drawn buggy, farm without power machines, and dress in plain dark clothes. Most Amish children attend one-room schoolhouses.

Illinois is one of five states with active Amish settlements. Modern residents of Arthur and Arcola respect Amish privacy and enjoy the products of Amish life. Stores carry Amish hand-carved furniture and needlework crafts. The closest Amish come to modern times is preparing white and fruit breads, pies, and cheeses for tourists, which they sell in their stores and restaurants.

SCHOOLS

Illinois schools include the best and worst in education. The best is seen in school districts that can afford extra programs, higher teacher salaries, and supplies to ensure quality education. They send children to the annual Young Authors Fair in Springfield, where the state honors hundreds of talented writers from around Illinois.

The worst lies in run-down city schools with boarded windows. Art, music, gym, and special writing programs, often a student's main school interests, are cut for lack of funds. Teachers receive few supplies, and kids read from old textbooks.

"This state and federal government underfund schools," says an angry inner-city teacher.

Illinois ranks thirty-fifth in school spending. In areas without enough money, as high as four of every ten children never finish high school. Statewide, the dropout rate is 10 percent, and national test scores are low.

Safety is a problem in many Illinois inner-city schools, too. Some principals hire off-duty police as guards. They lock doors during school hours and use metal detectors to search kids for guns. Several schools ban hats or earrings that suggest gangs.

One in six Illinois families turn to nonpublic schools for their children. Illinois' largest private school system is run by the Roman Catholic church. Even the church, however, abandons schools in poor neighborhoods when money is tight.

When the church threatened to close Providence St. Mel, principal Paul Adams fought back. He ran a tough but safe school for Chicago inner-city students. Adams became the school's devoted fund-raiser, teacher, bus driver, and gardener. When robbers broke in, he moved into the school as well.

Chicago's Oprah Winfrey celebrated Adams and his school in a television special. His greatest achievement is the overwhelming number (99 percent) of graduates from gang-infested neighborhoods who go on to college.

"We expect you to be the best and competitive," he tells new students. "We expect you to make this a better world. You are special."

Illinois has an outstanding network of colleges and universities. The University of Illinois' main campus in Champaign-Urbana brings together more than thirty-six thousand students from fifty states and one hundred nations. More than nine state-supported universities operate throughout Illinois, including a network of colleges and junior colleges in the Chicago area.

"Most people think Illinois is for farmers only," explains fundraiser Judy Checker. "They aren't aware of the research firsts from here."

So many supercomputer advances were developed at the Urbana campus that East Central Illinois became known as the "Silicon Prairie." Illinois was the first major university to provide programs for students with disabilities, including opportunities for Sharon Hedrick (gold in 1984 and 1988) and Jean Driscoll (silver in 1992) to win Special Olympic gold medals for wheelchair racing.

Illinois residents are crazy about their private colleges too. When Northwestern University's football team went to the Rose Bowl in 1996 for the first time in thirty-seven years, all of Evanston went wild. Jacksonville residents quickly point out that MacMurray College offered the first advanced degrees to women in the nation. And nearby Illinois College, an important station along the Underground Railroad, teaches state-of-the-art methods for working with children who are deaf.

Equally impressive are the more than fifty Nobel Prize winners from the University of Chicago and Chicago's north side Native American College, NACE (Native American Community for Education), the only Midwest school devoted to preserving tribal culture. Illinois offers hope for the future through its many first-rate schools.

5 THE BEST AND THE BRIGHTEST

"I loved the prairie," said celebrated architect Frank Lloyd Wright, "the trees, flowers, and sky were thrilling by contrast."

Illinois has touched the lives of many famous people. It is a place where anyone can succeed and anything can happen—creative entertainment, unusual inventions and buildings, surprising sports—and much already has.

MUSIC

Illinois is a great state for music. Almost every type of sound can be heard in theaters, clubs, stadiums, and free recitals. Chicago's Soldier Field and Champaign's mushroom-shaped assembly hall hold large rock concerts. Smaller theaters stage musicals and classical performances.

Downstaters listen to twangy country tunes. Country music is the mainstay at state and county fairs. Further north, singers in city clubs mix country rhythms with folk and rock music.

Chicago's Mayor Richard Daley likes plain country music. In 1991, he suggested that the city hold a country festival. But Chicago lawmakers preferred classical or jazz. The idea died. Instead, a country festival became part of the city's Taste of Chicago festival.

The Chicago Symphony Orchestra and Chicago Symphony Chorus perform to sellout crowds during winters. Both fill downtown Orchestra Hall with magical sounds. By summer, the world-class orchestra moves outdoors to Ravinia in suburban Highland Park.

The music that best represents Illinois, however, is jazz and blues. "This is a place for music and a great place for jazz—that's why I've been here all these years," says jazz pianist Ramsey Lewis.

African Americans first brought jazz from the South during the early 1900s. Some jazz beats combined with church gospel music. What came out was the longing sounds of blues. Both free-spirited rhythms caught on.

Then Louis "Satchmo" Armstrong's trumpet added his exciting sounds in Chicago. Musicians came from around the country to play Chicago-style jazz with him. American sailors carried jazz and blues overseas. Chicago blues became the starting point for new music in Europe.

Homegrown talent is what really made this music so popular. Clarinet player Benny Goodman first played in Hull House as a child. As an adult, he performed his own style of jazz, called swing. Goodman's band included black and white musicians, a brave move for the 1930s. At dance halls or on records and radio, everyone listened to the "King of Swing." In 1985, a year before he died, Goodman received a Grammy Award for his musical gifts to the world.

Every June, Moline hosts the Mississippi Valley Blues Fest. Musicians like Moline saxophonist Eddie Shaw and Muddy Waters keep the blues alive. Ravinia, which mainly played classical music, now has an annual jazz festival.

Louis "Satchmo" Armstrong became famous for clear high trumpet notes and hot jazz he played in Chicago.

Chicago holds its own separate jazz and blues festivals. They are part of the yearly free concert series at Grant Park. Illinois jazz and blues clubs attract musicians and listeners from across the nation. Illinois remains the capital of rhythm and blues.

FUNNY PEOPLE

Few people think of Illinois as a funny place. Yet, Illinois cartoonists and comedians have tickled the nation's funny bone for decades.

Arcola's Johnny Gruelle first drew the characters Raggedy Ann and Andy to go with his daughter's bedtime stories. Then she died at age three. The sad artist wrote his stories down as a way to feel better. Gruelle believed that happy books made children—and adults—feel good. Today, millions of delighted youngsters fall asleep cuddling stuffed toys made from Gruelle's characters. Each summer, Arcola holds a Raggedy Ann Festival to honor Gruelle and his lovable characters.

Elzie Segar modeled Popeye, Wimpy, and Olive Oil cartoon characters after his Chester neighbors. Today, the spinach-popping strong man decorates the town water tower and a huge statue. A fast-food hamburger chain calls itself Wimpy after Segar's chubby character who loved burgers. Segar's hometown of Chester has a Popeye museum store and national fan club of 650 members.

"We also organize an annual Popeye festival." says museum owner and Popeye lover Debbie Brooks.

The most famous Illinois cartoonist is Walt Disney . He was born in Chicago and moved out of state. But he returned to study art, so Illinoisans claim him as their own. Disney created Donald Duck, Mickey Mouse, and a host of other funny cartoons for books and movies.

Making people laugh is part of Illinois culture. Many said Abe Lincoln was a man who could "make a cat laugh." During the 1970s, Richard Pryor made a career of telling funny stories about his painful upbringing in Peoria. Today, Second City continues the tradition.

When this comedy company formed in 1959, Illinois theater consisted of traveling New York shows. New Yorkers joked that

Walt Disney drew Mickey Mouse, the cartoon that won him a 1932 Academy Award.

Chicago was second to their city in every form of entertainment, especially theater. A group of Chicago actors accepted the challenge. Moreover, they called their comedy group Second City. The name was the company's first joke—on New York.

Second City developed Chicago's special form of humor, improvisation. Improv, for short, is spur-of-the-moment. Kids improvise all the time when they play house, school, or superheros. Second City actors wanted to tap into this childhood skill. After each show, they would ask the audience for suggestions of what they should act out.

"The cast works up scenes from these germs of ideas," explains

Second City's Audrey Pass. "The good ones are put into the our regular show."

Second City set many standards for comedy, expanding to Toronto, Canada, and Detroit. Shortly after, a comedy club craze blossomed in Chicago and other big cities. Second City prepared actors for movies and television, especially *Saturday Night Live*. Bill Murray of Evanston and Dan Akroyd (*Ghostbusters*), Laurie Metcalfe (*Roseanne*), and Harold Ramis (*Honey I Shrunk the Kids*) were all Second City graduates. Chicagoan Robin Williams followed the company's crazy, free-form style.

Chicago-born comic Robin Williams dressed in costume for the opening of his movie "Toys."

According to the *Chicago Tribune,* "There are few things we find funny that can't be traced back to some Second City source."

ARCHITECTURE

Historic landmarks can be found throughout the Illinois. Grand court houses have beautified town squares for more than one hundred years. Their splendor recalls each towns' special past. Statehouses in Vandalia and Springfield display carefully crafted classical styles that are rarely seen today. Huge marble buildings throughout Springfield highlight the city's place as center of government.

The highlight of Illinois architecture, however, is in Chicago. The Chicago School of Architecture is world famous. Such architects as Louis Sullivan and Daniel Burnham created landmarks from the ashes of the Chicago Fire of 1871. Burnham ordered, "Make no little plans: they have no magic to stir men's minds."

Chicago architects changed building design with their use of steel beams and glass. Endless possibilities unfolded once they replaced heavy 18th-century stone walls. William Le Baron Jenney built the first skyscraper with a metal frame. In 1885, his ten-story Home Insurance Building became a model for future skyscrapers. Today, the Rookery by Burnham and John Welborn Root stands as the world's oldest remaining steel-framed sky-scraper.

A big part of the Chicago School includes the works of Oak Park architect Frank Lloyd Wright. He believed buildings should fit their surroundings. Therefore, he designed buildings low and wide like

Illinois' prairie, rather than skyscraper tall. He used bricks and woods that blended into landscapes. His stained glass windows pictured colorful prairie flowers and grasses.

Wright's buildings became known as the "Prairie Style." They are sprinkled throughout the Midwest. Oak Park has more Wright buildings than any other town. Wright, who lived in Oak Park for twenty-two years, built twenty-five structures there during his first two decades as an architect.

German-American architect Ludwig Mies van der Rohe revived the high-rise tradition during the 1940s. By then, Chicago had the world's largest commercial center. But New York skyscrapers had topped Chicago's turn-of-the-century building heights. Van der Rohe achieved a new look with glass and steel. He created tall apartment buildings with simple, straight lines, a first anywhere. "Less is more" was his motto.

Downtown Chicago features four soaring skyscrapers. Everyone likes to pick out the 110-story Sears Tower in the downtown skyline. At 1,450 feet, it is among the tallest in the world. The building is 325 feet higher than "Big John," Chicago's John Hancock Center. The Sears Tower is even taller than the World Trade Center in New York—another reason Chicago is no "second city."

SPORTS

In the early 1900s, Chicago Board of Education president Otto Schneider called high school sports a "national disease." But his belief never slowed Illinoisan interest in sports. Local elementary,

high school, and college sports draw devoted fans for basketball, soccer, baseball, football, and hockey. Individual sports, such as swimming, gymnastics, figure skating, and track and field provide hours of fun for Illinois athletes.

Chicago professional teams receive the most attention. The city has two major-league baseball teams—the Cubs and White Sox. Both have a poor record. The only two World Series the Cubs ever won were in 1907 and 1908. Still, Illinois baseball fans stay loyal for life.

"I can't understand why my brother loves the Cubs even though they never win," says a suburban woman with a shrug.

The state has a strong history of minority baseball leagues. Baseball teams, like the Champaign Eagles, played with the Negro Baseball League in the days before blacks were allowed into major-league teams.

Women's baseball blossomed in Illinois during World War II. At the time, chewing gum king Philip Wrigley owned the Chicago Cubs. He started the All-American Girls Professional Baseball League to keep fans interested while his players served in the war. Women in lipstick and short skirts dazzled audiences with their pitching and batting. By the time the league ended in 1954, there were ten teams, including the famous Rockford Peaches from the movie, *A League of Their Own.*

Today, three teams of Illinois women play baseball with the American Women's Baseball Association. The Gators, Daredevils,

Chicago's downtown skyline sparkles with lights from the Sears Tower (center) and surrounding office buildings.

Rockford Peaches manager and former ice hockey star, Eddie Stumpf, gives his team a pep talk. The 1940s baseball players are (left to right) Elise Harney, Lois Florreich, Mille Warwick, Olive Little, and Dottie Green.

and Knights have been batting at the Kane County Stadium in Geneva since 1988.

Most people never knew that softball began in Illinois. Chicagoan George W. Hancock invented the game in 1887 as an indoor sport. The first ball was seventeen inches, then twelve, and finally sixteen. The game became so popular that the Amateur Softball Association formed in 1933.

The Chicago Bulls play basketball to sellout crowds. Their following exploded after two years of National Basketball Association (NBA) playoff wins. Their success expanded general interest in local basketball. Fans began to follow college teams, such as the Northwestern Women's Wildcats.

Chicago Bears football tickets used to be passed from one generation to another. For decades, the self-important team threatened to leave Chicago for a better stadium in the suburbs, and hopefully more wins. By 1995, interest was down after a terrible losing streak. Mayor Daley grew tired of the team's threats and said "They can go to Alaska."

Illinois towns admire their sports stars. In Chicago's inner city that includes the Jesse White Tumblers. State representative Jesse White began the gymnastics group in 1959. He wanted to give inner city kids a chance to feel good about themselves. Today, the kids perform at basketball halftimes and special events nationwide.

According to teen tumbler Greg Bogan, "When it starts getting dark out, all the gangs come out. We stay away from that. That's why we got into tumbling."

East St. Louis claims the Olympic track star Jackie Joyner-Kersee. In 1988, she earned two gold medals. One was for the long jump, and the other a contest that included seven track events. Some believe she is the greatest woman runner.

Similarly, Champaign fans love lightening-quick ice skater Bonnie Blair. Blair was born in New York, but she went to the University of Illinois and has lived here ever since. In 1988, she received a gold medal for the 500-meter speed skating competition. During the 1992 Olympics, Blair earned a double gold medal in the 500- and 1000-meter races.

Far and away, the most popular athlete in Illinois is Bulls

Bonnie Blair won the women's
500-meter speed skating
Olympic gold metal in 1994.
She became the first speed
skater to win a gold metal in
the same event for three
Winter Olympics in a row.

In 1987, Jackie Joyner-Kersee tied
the world long jump record of 24
feet 5 1/2 inches.

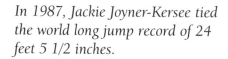

basketball star Michael Jordan. Jordan earned seven scoring titles, led the Bulls to three national championships in a row, and helped the U.S. Olympic team win a gold medal. His graceful leaps seem to suspend his body in the air as he shoots difficult baskets. The Bulls placed a statue of him in front of the new Chicago Stadium. Even people uninterested in sports make time to watch Jordan.

Michael Jordan easily won a slam-dunk contest in Chicago for the second year in 1988. No one flies like Jordan!

GREAT ADVENTURES IN SCIENCE, ENGINEERING, AND THE IMAGINATION

Illinois author L. Frank Baum published the *Wonderful Wizard of Oz* in Chicago in 1900. This popular book inspired a movie and a statue of Baum in Chicago's Lincoln Park. The story told of young Dorothy and her dog Toto's adventures. On their journey, they overcame scary events by being clever, and they reached exciting places. Similar paths have been traveled by many creative Illinoisans.

In September 1992, doctor and engineer Mae Jemison took the greatest adventure of her life. She traveled from Chicago's south side, where she was raised, into space on the shuttle Endeavour. "I recall looking up at the stars, knowing I'd go up there some day," Jemison said about her childhood.

Jemison was the first black woman in outer space. Today, she uses space technology to improve the health of poor West Africans. She also teaches students in America "not to be limited by others' limited imaginations."

George Pullman imagined a new kind of train travel. In 1858, the Bloomington engineer built the first usable railroad sleeping car. Shortly after, he designed the first dining car, complete with a kitchen and parlor area. His visions changed railroad travel forever. He became a millionaire with the Pullman Palace Car Company and established Pullman, a factory town for his railroad workers on Chicago's south side. The historic town of Pullman still stands as a reminder of the area's industrial peak.

Galesburg engineer George Ferris had a great vision, too. He built a huge moving wheel in Chicago for the 1893 Columbian Exposi-

ILLINOIS POET GWENDOLYN BROOKS

Chicago poet Gwendolyn Brooks was the first black to win a Pulitzer Prize in 1950. She has been the state Poet Laureate since 1968, following Carl Sandburg. Brooks enjoys reading her poems to school children throughout Illinois. The children she meets often inspire her poetry. This one from Children Coming Home was for Diego and all children of color.

PUZZLEMENT:
"BLACK PRIDE" DAY

I, partly Nigerian.
I, partly Puerto Rican.

I have a Nigerian father,
a Puerto Rican mother.
I am packed in a skin that is tan.

I, too, have a heart on fire.
I, too, want to be Proud.
I, too, want to be Something and Proud.

I want to shout "I'M A TAN!"

The 1893 World's Columbian Exposition in Chicago began before crews finished the giant "Observation Wheel." Today, this fifteen-story Ferris wheel is a main attraction at the amusement park on Chicago's renovated Navy Pier.

tion, the first World's Fair in the United States. His Observation Wheel was twenty-six stories tall and sparkled with three thousand lights. It was high enough to "observe" the entire fair. Each of 36 cars held 60 standing people, a total of 2,160 riders for each 20-minute trip.

Inventor and engineer William E. Sullivan of Roodhouse rode on the wheel at the 1904 St. Louis Fair. Sullivan's mind spun with exciting plans for a smaller Ferris Wheel that could be moved easily. He returned home and created the first Big Wheel with twelve seats, each for three people.

Engineer friends laughed at the idea, much as Ferris' friends laughed at him. They said he should stick with building bridges. So Sullivan called his new business Eli Bridge Company. That way people would give money for his 1906 Jacksonville factory, even though they thought the wheel was silly.

Eli Bridge Company is the oldest and largest ferris wheel factory anywhere. The current president, William A. Sullivan, is the fourth generation of Sullivans to head the company, the longest-running in Jacksonville. He sells wheels worldwide for carnivals, fairs, and amusement parks.

"Entertainer Michael Jackson has one in Neverland," says Sullivan proudly. "I delivered, built, and tested that wheel. It's an honor to continue the Eli legacy. As my father once said, 'We may not be making . . . rocket ships that go to the moon, but our products sure bring joy to a lot of people. Especially little people. And that's important, too.'"

6 ILLINOIS HIGHLIGHTS

Matteson State Park

"I love it here," beams one newcomer from the East Coast. "The state combines the hectic pace of big eastern cities like Philadelphia with southern gentility. The people look at you and make eye contact: they're really friendly."

Touring Illinois is a treat. With good trains, highways, and airports, traveling is easier here than in many places. And people around the state welcome visitors with easy smiles and goodwill. They are proud to tell you about where they live.

CHICAGO

"When I lived in Atlanta, I felt I was living in the state of Georgia," notes an Ohio-born author. "In Illinois, I have the feeling of living in Chicago."

For many people, Illinois *is* Chicago. It is the nation's third largest city. Chicago has a majority of the state's production and much of the population. Colorful ethnic neighborhoods, grand monuments, festivals, parks, beaches, and museums rival any in the world. With the bustle of big business and downtown shopping streets, people never get bored.

"The best part of living in Illinois is the city of Chicago as the center of culture," observes tour guide Steve Berger.

Any type of entertainment can be found here. Dance companies, such as the lively Hubbard Street, the Chicago Symphony, theLyric Opera, and many theaters and clubs offer enjoyment for every taste. Sports lovers watch professional team events and Special Olympics in large stadiums and play polo and volleyball along the lakefront.

One hundred years ago, city planners developed Chicago's twenty-nine miles of shoreline into a tree-lined skyline of parks, museums, and recreation areas. On hot summer days, people flock from every neighborhood to cool off at lakefront beaches. They picnic, rollerblade, bicycle, fish, golf, and jog. Many families crowd Lincoln Park Zoo, one of the few free big-city zoos left.

Downtown's Grant Park is the city's "front lawn." Summer nights are for free music concerts. After the music, colorful dancing lights spout from nearby Buckingham Fountain. Almost every summer weekend, the park comes alive with festivals that showcase local gifts—gospel, bagpipers, jazz, blues, and Latin beats.

"Over one million people celebrate our beautiful lakefront at Venetian Night. For almost forty years, viewers delighted to the parade of decorated boats and following fireworks," notes a city worker.

Grant Park is home to many outstanding museums. One of the oldest collections is in the Field Museum of Natural History. Its exhibits of mummies and dinosaurs were part of the 1893 world's fair. The museum invites families for yearly sleepovers. Late at night, when lights are low, creepy lifelike creatures watch kids eat snacks and curl into sleeping bags.

The Art Institute of Chicago was actually built during the fair.

GANGSTER HIDEOUTS

Chicago has its share of unusual buildings. At 35 West Wacker Drive, the office tower was once a jewelers building with an elevator big enough to hold a car. That way, the jewelers could drive their cars upstairs without worrying about getting robbed.

Feared gangster, Al Capone, used the upper four floors for a hang-out during the 1920s. It was illegal at the time to buy and sell alcohol throughout the United States. Capone's cruel empire of criminals made and sold liquor. He opened a lively speakeasy, a private drinking club, on the top floor. Anyone who objected was kidnapped, beaten, or killed. Capone finally went to jail for not paying enough taxes. Even then, his mother claimed he was a "good boy."

For years, the murderous Capone gang was all people remembered about Illinois.

Since then, the museum has assembled a world-famous collection of paintings, sculpture, and crafts. Even kids who dislike museums love the weekend art projects, armor collection, and Thorne miniature rooms. Wide-eyed kids wonder how to make such tiny chairs or tables look like real furniture from long ago.

Chicago's downtown business district is an outdoor museum of architecture. This area is called the Loop after the elevated train tracks that ring or "loop" the district. The Loop showcases fresh ideas in building that keep the Chicago School of Architecture alive. Modern architects top their buildings with beehives, geometric designs, or domes that look like plastic bags.

Wide plazas between grand office buildings feature sculpture from the most famous world artists. Claes Oldenburg, who taught at the Art Institute, created the sporty gray "Bat Column," a hollow metal baseball bat, in front of a federal building. Spanish artist Pablo Picasso gave Chicago a huge metal sculpture for Civic Center plaza. After decades, passers-by still ask, "What is that?"

Light-hearted sculptures are sprinkled throughout downtown and lakefront parks. The northwest suburb of Skokie liked Chicago's idea of art everyone can enjoy. City leaders created sculpture gardens in the park along the Chicago River and in Old Orchard shopping mall.

Chicago continues to recycle its relics. Warehouses become indoor golf courses, restaurants and museums. The lakefront's three-quarter-mile long Navy Pier is a lively lakefront playground. It contains the Children's Museum, three-dimensional movie theater, carousel, and outdoor stages. A 15-story Ferris wheel with 16,000 lights overlooks the harbor, and Chicago skyline.

Picasso's unusual gift to Chicago was one of the first outdoor plaza sculptures in the city.

On north Michigan Avenue is the "Magnificent Mile," a stretch of elegant shops. Off the main street is a city visitor center. This historic Water Tower is in the only remaining building from the great Chicago fire. Each winter holiday season, the street shimmers with thousands of white lights. They beckon adventurers who seek the city's night-life on nearby Rush Street.

Farther west is the Peace Museum. This is the only art and history museum dedicated to peace. Art, music, and writing

FIESTA DE SOL

According to Helen Valdez, founder of the Mexican Fine Arts Center Museum in the Pilsen neighborhood, Chicago has "the fastest-growing population of Latinos" in the United States. For five days each summer, the community holds Fiesta de Sol to honor their culture. Fiesta de Sol has one hundred booths with foods rides, and crafts—a carnival atmosphere. It is the biggest Mexican festival in the United States.

exhibits about world peace come and go. But the museum is the permanent home of an eighteen-mile "peace ribbon" from the 1986 Ribbon Project. Children and adults nationwide created cloth banners to wrap around the Pentagon in Washington, D.C., the place where government decides matters of war and peace.

Chicago is a city of neighborhoods. Unlike the suburbs where cars and shopping malls rule, Chicagoans travel by foot, bus, and public train. Neighborhoods reveal their own personality in the houses, stores, food smells, libraries, and language in the streets. Jane Addams Hull House is still open as a museum near the University of Illinois, a monument to neighborhood cooperation.

Author Andrew Greeley wrote how "you have to poke around the neighborhoods to know Chicago."

On the south side is 543 acres of Jackson Park, site of the 1893 fair. The giant stone Museum of Science and Industry reminds visitors of how grand the event was. Today, the museum exhibits a World War II submarine, coal mine, and a real 727 jet plane. With more than 4 million visitors a year, this is the city's most popular museum.

Nearby Hyde Park boasts higher learning at the stately University of Chicago campus. Perhaps that's why the community hosts a large book fair each year. The Du Sable Museum of African American History traces black roots in Chicago, beginning with the city's first settler.

Closer downtown is Spanish-speaking Pilsen near Harrison Park. An orange steel abstract Puerto Rican flag waves over Division Street. A converted boat repair shop houses the country's largest museum dedicated to Mexican culture, the Mexican Fine Arts Center Museum.

The city and suburbs celebrate their ethnic roots with music, food, crafts, parades, and carnivals. Greek town, Little Italy, Andersonville, and Chinatown each contain blocks of active restaurants that feature their nationality's food. Evanston holds an Ethnic Fair for every group. Russian stacking dolls mingle with Nicaraguan hammocks. African dancers bounce to pounding drums.

During the late 1800s, a New Yorker called Chicago the "Windy City." People thought the name suggested the gusty winds that blow off Lake Michigan. The man really referred to the "windy" Chicagoans who brag so much about their city.

NORTHERN ILLINOIS

Suburbs seem to extend Chicago forever. Chicago-style comedy, music, and theater have blossomed far from their downtown Chicago homes. In addition, each community celebrates its own

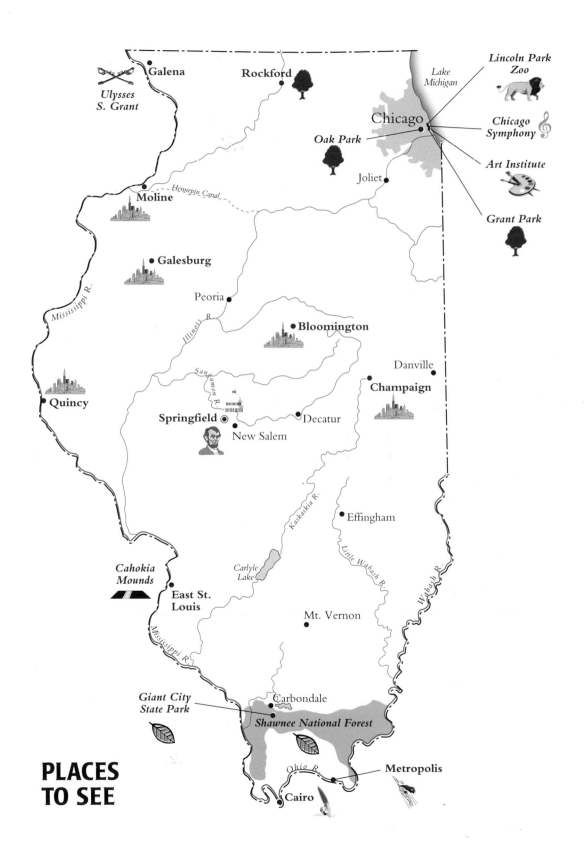

Galena
Rockford

Ulysses S. Grant

Lincoln Park Zoo

Lake Michigan

Chicago

Chicago Symphony

Oak Park

Joliet

Art Institute

Grant Park

Hennepin Canal

Moline

Galesburg

Peoria

Illinois R.

Bloomington

Danville

Mississippi R.

Quincy

Sangamon R.

Champaign

Springfield

Decatur

New Salem

Kaskaskia R.

Effingham

Little Wabash R.

Wabash R.

Cahokia Mounds

Carlyle Lake

East St. Louis

Mt. Vernon

Mississippi R.

Giant City State Park

Carbondale

Shawnee National Forest

Ohio R.

Metropolis

Cairo

PLACES TO SEE

Visitors flock to celebrate Chinese New Year in Chicago's Chinatown. A colorful parade ends with delicious treats from local restaurants.

hometown heros and history. Oak Park holds a Hemingway Festival to remember where author Ernest Hemingway was born. Guides take tours through buildings designed by architect Frank Lloyd Wright.

Ninety minutes northwest of Chicago is Rockford, Illinois' second largest city. The town began in 1834 when a dam was built over the Rock River for a sawmill. The "Rock ford" offered travelers a way to cross the river between Chicago and Galena. The name stuck.

Rockford is mainly a manufacturing city. There are a few museums and an annual riverfront festival. The main attraction, however, is trees. Rockford averages one hundred trees for every city block. Citizens call their home "The City of Trees."

Train nuts go to nearby Union to the Illinois Railway Museum. They can see 250 cars and locomotives, including the last Chicago streetcar to run in 1958. Most visitors prefer to boat, fish, and camp in the regions more than 160 parks.

Galena recreates the history of northwest Illinois. This "is the town that time forgot." The clock stopped during the 1850s when Galena was a mining and riverboat boomtown of 15,000 people and Chicago only a clump of cabins.

Today, the area's four thousand residents embrace life as it was. Much of the main street has been restored. Most of the town's old mansions and buildings are national historic sites. The house that the city awarded to Civil War hero General Ulysses S. Grant is a major tourist stop. Folk singer Jim Post performs the one-person show "Galena Rose" in the old Trolley Depot Theater. His songs preserve Galena's past.

CENTRAL ILLINOIS

"Kids from Jacksonville take Lincoln stuff for granted," remembers Becky Todd. "Their field trips are to Springfield, Lincoln's Tomb, and New Salem. They often don't understand why visitors from other states are interested in Lincoln places."

Central Illinois is the Land of Lincoln. The region has more historic sites than all others in the state combined. This is due in part to Springfield being the state capital, but mostly, because Lincoln lived, worked, and was buried in central Illinois.

New Salem along the Sangamon River was where Lincoln lived from 1831 to 1837. In 1933 a federal program recreated the town on its original foundation. Today, the village gives a clear idea of Lincoln's time, as guides tell secrets about Lincoln and his neighbors. They dress in puffy-sleeved dresses with awkward billowy skirts and warm buckskin pants with rabbit caps, even in summer. They explain what it was like to spend your whole life— eat, sleep, cook, sew—in one room, sometimes shared with animals.

Fifteen miles away is Springfield. The only home Lincoln ever owned is on Jackson and 8th streets. His law offices are nearby. Furnishings are a combination of what the family owned and what they might have sold before leaving. The home's parlor is set up for adult-only events, such as popular "strawberry parties," when friends gathered to eat strawberries and cream.

Springfield has several grand state buildings. Lincoln argued more than two hundred cases before the Illinois Supreme court in the Old State Capitol. But the State Capitol begun in 1868 is the current hub of government.

The Capitol extends three city blocks and is seventy-four feet taller than the national Capitol. Each picture, marking, and statue captures an important feature in Illinois history, such as the statue of the first woman state legislator in 1922, Lottie Holman O'Neill. Pictures of Abraham Lincoln and Stephen Douglas on different sides of the House chamber show lawmakers where to sit. Republicans sit on Lincoln's side, and Democrats sit on Douglas' side.

Mary Todd and Abraham Lincoln bought their Springfield house for $1,200. Lincoln chopped the wood, carried the water, and milked the cow to keep expenses down.

Outside of Springfield is Lincoln's tomb in Oak Ridge Cemetery. He is buried with Mary and three of their sons. On the walls are carved Lincoln's most famous speeches. One tells of the new president leaving his beloved home. He said of his Springfield neighbors, "to the kindest of these people I owe everything."

Hikers can almost hear the Native Americans speak of the old ways as they walk through the Garden of the Gods.

SOUTHERN ILLINOIS

At first, the girls at Mt. Vernon's Wheels Through Time Museum just smiled. "You want to know what we do for fun? Well," laughed one of them, "we have frog races for excitement."

Then they thought some more, and their pride swelled about southern Illinois. The greatest treasure they agreed was in the Shawnee National Forest. "You've got to see the Garden of the Gods," they exclaimed. The ancient rock formation was a favorite place where teenagers climbed.

"And you must walk through Giant City," they continued. These rock designs were part of the larger Giant City State Park. The park was named for the huge rock walls that look like shaded streets. Native Americans lived in the bluffs almost ten thousand years ago. Blackened ceilings from their fires can still be seen today.

The most striking reminder of Indian life is Cahokia Mounds Historic Site near East St. Louis. An interesting movie, dioramas, and live demonstrations at the visitor center bring Native American history to life. Then the fun starts—exploring the mounds on foot and imagining what Illinois was like more than nine hundred years ago.

Illinois has more wonderful treasures than one book can discover. People of the original "Prairie State" and historic "Land of Lincoln" would most likely agree that, as Frank Baum wrote in *The Wizard of Oz,* "There's no place like home."

ILLINOIS

THE FLAG: The state flag, which shows the state seal on a white background, was first adopted in 1915.   The state name was added in 1969.

THE SEAL: In the center of the state seal is an American eagle holding a shield with stars and stripes for the 13 original states. The eagle holds a banner with the state's motto in its beak. Olive branches under the shield symbolize peace. A nearby boulder has two dates: 1818, the year Illinois entered the Union, and 1868, the year the seal was adopted.

STATE SURVEY

Statehood: December 3, 1818

Origin of Name: Illinois is French for Iliniwek, the name of the group of Native Americans who lived in the region before the coming of white settlers.

Nickname: Prairie State, Land of Lincoln

Capital: Springfield

Motto: State Sovereignty, National Union

Bird: Cardinal

Animal: White-tailed deer

Fish: Bluegill

Insect: Monarch butterfly

Flower: Native violet

Tree: White oak

Mineral: Fluorite

GEOGRAPHY

Highest Point: 1,235 feet above sea level, at Charles Mound

Lowest Point: 279 feet above sea level, along the Mississippi River in southern Illinois

STATE SONG

Illinois had considered "Illinois" its state song from the time it was written by Charles H. Chamberlain sometime between 1890 and 1893. Chamberlain had set his words to a melody written by Archibald Johnson in 1870, in hopes that his lyrics coupled with Johnson's familiar tune would help bring the 1893 World's Columbian Exposition to Chicago. In 1925, State Senator Florence Fifer Bohner, the first woman to hold a seat in the Illinois Senate, introduced a motion to proclaim "Illinois" the official state song. It was adopted on June 25, 1925.

Area: 55,645 square miles

Greatest Distance, North to South: 385 miles

Greatest Distance, East to West: 220 miles

Bordering States: Wisconsin to the north, Iowa and Missouri to the south-west, Kentucky to the south-east, and Indiana to the east

Hottest Recorded Temperature: 117°F at East St. Louis on July 14, 1954

Coldest Recorded Temperature: −35°F at Mount Carroll on January 22, 1930

Average Annual Precipitation: 38 inches

Major Rivers: Mississippi, Illinois, Wabash, Chicago, Des Plaines, Rock, Vermilion, Fox, Sangamon, Spoon, Kankakee, Embarras, Big Muddy, Kaskaskia, Pecatonica, Calumet, Kishwaukee

Major Lakes: Michigan, Carlyle, Crab Orchard, Rend, Chain O'Lakes Goose, Peoria, Senachwine, Springfield, Decatur, Bloomington, Lake of Egypt, Shelbyville

Trees: oak, white oak, hickory, elm, ash, cottonwood, walnut, maple birch, beech, sycamore, bald cypress, tupelo gum

Wild Plants: violet, wild barley, gumweed, wild geranium, bluebell, chess, bloodroot, Dutchman's-breeches, toothwort, snow trillium, goldenrod

Animals: white-tailed deer, squirrel, rabbit, raccoon, fox, beaver, opossum, skunk, mink, muskrat

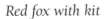 *Red fox with kit*

Birds: cardinal, sparrow, bluejay, American crow, chickadee, red-winged blackbird, hummingbird, bobwhite quail, ringneck pheasant, Canada goose

Fish: bluegill, carp, catfish, largemouth and smallmouth bass, red-ear sunfish, crappie, perch, white bass, walleye, sauger, bullhead, buffalo fish, northern pike, salmon, lake trout

Endangered Animals: gray bat, Indiana bat, river otter, eastern wood rat, white-tailed jackrabbit, double-crested cormorant, snowy egret, little blue heron, osprey, bald eagle, peregrine falcon, northern harrier, sandhill crane, piping plover, least tern, barn owl, yellow-headed blackbird, pallid sturgeon, bigeye chub, cypress minnow, western sand darter, silvery salamander, Illinois mud turtle, spotted turtle, broad-banded watersnake, eastern ribbon snake, rattlesnake master moth, Iowa Pleistocene snail, Arogos skipper butterfly, white wartyback pearly (mussel), rough pigtoe (mussel), white cat's paw pearly (mussel)

Barn owl nestlings

Endangered Plants: Mead's milkweed, Decurrent false aster, lakeside daisy, prairie bush-clover, eastern prairie fringed orchid, leafy prairie clover

TIMELINE

Illinois History

c. 1500 The Iliniweks live in the region that will become Illinois

1673 Jolliet and Marquette explore Illinois

1680 La Salle builds Fort Crevecoeur near the present site of Peoria

1699 Settlement of Cahokia founded

1703 Settlement of Kaskaskia founded

1763 British troops enter Illinois and take control of the region from the French

1778 George Rogers Clark captures Kaskaskia from the British

1779 Du Sable constructs a trading post at the present-day site of Chicago

1779 Settlers from Maryland and Virginia establish the first English-speaking settlement in Illinois, near present-day Waterloo

1787 Illinois becomes part of the Northwest Territory according to the Northwest Ordinance, in which Congress rules that the region will eventually be divided into a number of states

1809 The Territory of Illinois created

1818 Illinois becomes a state

1832 The Black Hawk War ends Native American resistance in Illinois

1834 Abraham Lincoln elected to the Illinois House of Representatives

1837 Illinois capital moves from Vandalia to Springfield

1858 Abraham Lincoln and Stephen A. Douglas hold a series of debates as they campaign for U.S. senator

1860 Abraham Lincoln elected President of the United States

1861 Civil War begins

1863 Emancipation Proclamation

1865 Lincoln assassinated and buried in Springfield

1869 Transcontinental railroad completed

1871 Great Chicago Fire

1886 Haymarket Riot in Chicago

1889 Jane Addams' Hull House opens in Chicago

1893 The World's Columbian Exposition opens in Chicago

1919 Race riots erupt in Chicago

1929 Great Depression begins

1933 A Century of Progress Exposition opens in Chicago

1968 Gwendolyn Brooks becomes poet laureate of Illinois

1971 Abraham Lincoln's Springfield home recognized as a national historic site

1973 The world's tallest building, the Sears Tower, completed in Chicago

1983 Harold Washington, Chicago's first black mayor, elected

1993 Millions of acres of Illinois farmland damaged by Mississippi flooding

ECONOMY

Agricultural Products: Corn, soybeans, wheat, oats, hay, apples, peaches, pumpkins, potatoes, hogs, cattle, dairy products, chickens, turkeys, eggs, sheep and lambs, minks

Manufactured Products: Construction machinery, printed products, farm machinery, electrical instruments, appliances, iron and steel, other metals, processed foods, meat products, railroad equipment, automobile parts chemicals, drugs

Natural Resources: Bituminous coal, crude oil, natural gas, fluorspar, tripoli, zinc, copper, lead, lime, silver, barite, clay, sand and gravel, crushed stone, peat, timber

Business and Trade: Banking, advertising and public relations, insurance, retail sales, transportation, research

CALENDAR OF CELEBRATIONS

Bald Eagle Days This two-day festival comes in late January or early February in Rock Island, as bald eagles migrate southward along the Mississippi. Visitors can see live eagles close up in the exhibit hall. Or, eagles can be viewed as they fly and glide along the Mississippi River.

Lincoln Birthday Weekend Every February, Springfield hosts a weekend full of events, including parades and lectures by scholars on Lincoln's life and achievements.

Dutch Days The Dutch heritage of Fulton is celebrated every May with wooden shoe dancing and a parade featuring traditional Dutch costumes.

Illinois St. Andrew Highland Games Every June, Downers Grove is the site of a festival celebrating the area's Scottish heritage. The festival features Scottish food, dancing, games, and fun.

Superman Celebration Metropolis, the "official home of Superman," hosts a Superman festival every June that includes a live, outdoor Superman show.

Old Canal Days The city of Lockport celebrates its history along the Illinois and Michigan Canal every June with carriage rides and canal walks.

Taste of Chicago Held every June, this celebration showcases all the fantastic foods Chicago has to offer.

Blues Festival The special strains of the blues fill Chicago's streets in June when the city celebrates its musical roots.

Fiesta de Hemingway A week-long festival is held every July in Oak Park, where the writer Ernest Hemingway was born.

Illinois State Fair August brings the State Fair to Springfield along with food, music, rides, racing pigs, a cow carved from butter, and lots of other fun attractions.

Sweet Corn Festival Held every summer in Mendota, a farming community about eighty miles west of Chicago, this August festival serves up about 160,000 ears of corn to visitors.

Jazz Festival Jazz sounds are celebrated every August in Chicago, where so many jazz musicians got their start.

Rediscover Cahokia Days Usually held in August, this festival at the Cahokia Mounds celebrates the heritage of the region's Native Americans with dancing and craft demonstrations.

Jordbruksdagarna This September farm festival in the Swedish community of Bishop Hill demonstrates how early settlers harvested crops, the kinds of games they played, and crafts from the 1850s.

Railsplitting Festival The town of Lincoln hosts this tribute to Abraham Lincoln in September. The festival includes a railsplitting contest in honor of Lincoln's legendary skill at splitting logs into fence rails.

Fort Crevecoeur Rendevouz Every September, fur trappers in buckskins paddle their canoes and fire their flintlock rifles in this festival held at the state historic site.

STATE STARS

Jane Addams (1860–1935) was born in Cedarville and attended Rockford College. Addams opened Hull House, a neighborhood settlement house that offered care and education to the inner-city poor, in Chicago in 1889 after seeing a similar settlement house in London, England. Addams also worked for world peace and in 1931 earned a Nobel Peace Prize for her efforts.

Philip Danforth Armour (1832–1901) helped make Chicago a leader in the meat-packing industry. He founded Armour & Company in 1867 and bragged about using "every part of the pig but the squeal" in his meat products.

Black Hawk (1767–1838) was a leader of the Sauk people. After he was forced to leave the state, Black Hawk returned with a group of his people in 1832, which led to the outbreak of the Black Hawk War. Defeated by U.S. militia, Black Hawk spent the rest of his life in Iowa.

Bonnie Blair (1964–   ) of Champaign began ice skating when she was two years old. Years of practice helped her become the first woman to earn back-to-back gold medals in Olympic speed skating. Blair won gold in the 1988 and 1992 Winter Olympic Games.

Gwendolyn Brooks (1917–   ) was the first African-American woman poet to win a Pulitzer prize. Brooks grew up in Chicago, and much of her poetry concerns the life of black Americans. In 1968, Brooks became poet laureate of Illinois.

Edgar Rice Burroughs (1875–1950), the creator of Tarzan, was born in Chicago. Burroughs wrote his first book about the "King of the Jungle" in 1912 and wrote 26 Tarzan books in all. Burroughs' character has since been featured in many movies and television programs.

Richard Daley (1902–1976) was born in Chicago and served as that city's mayor for 21 years, from 1955 until his death. Daley was one of the most powerful politicians in America. He controlled Chicago government completely during his years in office.

Miles Davis (1926–1991) is known as one of the world's greatest jazz trumpet players. Born in Alton, Davis had a great influence on jazz styles in the 1950s and 1960s.

John Deere (1804–1886), a blacksmith born in Vermont, invented the first successful steel plow in his workshop in Grand Detour. Deere created his plow from an old saw blade after hearing local farmers complain that Illinois' thick soil stuck to their iron and wood plows. Deere's invention improved farming throughout the Midwest.

Walt Disney (1901–1966), the creator of Mickey Mouse and Disneyland, was born in Chicago. Although Disney moved from Illinois as a young boy, he returned to study art in Chicago. Among his many full-length animated films are *Snow White and the Seven Dwarfs, Cinderella,* and *Fantasia.*

Stephen A. Douglas (1813–1861), called "the Little Giant," is best known for his senate campaign against Abraham Lincoln in 1858. Douglas moved from Vermont to Illinois in 1833, served in the U.S. House of Representatives from 1843 to 1847, and then in the Senate from 1847 to 1861.

Jean Baptiste Point du Sable (1745–1818) was born in Haiti and was part African and part French. In 1779, du Sable became Chicago's first settler when he built a trading post at the mouth of the Chicago River. Although his trading post was very successful, du Sable mysteriously moved away in 1800.

George Ferris (1859–1896), the person after whom the Ferris wheel is named, was born in Galesburg. Ferris built a "pleasure wheel" that stood 264 feet high for the World's Columbian Exposition in Chicago in 1893. Such pleasure wheels soon came to be known as Ferris wheels.

Marshall Field (1834–1906) opened the Marshall Field & Company store in Chicago. Based on fair pricing and the slogan, "Give the Lady What She Wants," the store became the largest retail establishment in the world. Field gave much back to the community, including $9 million to open the Field Museum of Natural History.

Harrison Ford (1942–   ), one of Hollywood's most popular actors, was born in Chicago. Ford starred in *Star Wars* and its two sequels. He also played Indiana Jones in *Raiders of the Lost Ark, Indiana Jones and the Temple of Doom,* and *Indiana Jones and the Last Crusade.*

Ernest Hemingway (1899–1961), one of the twentieth century's greatest American authors, was born in Oak Park. Hemingway wrote both novels and short stories and received the 1954 Nobel Prize in literature. Some of his best-known works include *A Farewell to Arms, For Whom the Bell Tolls,* and *The Old Man and the Sea.*

Mahalia Jackson (1911–1972) moved to Chicago when she was 15 years old. A year later, she began singing gospel music and became one of the most popular gospel performers in history. Her million-selling songs include "Move on Up a Little Higher," and "He's Got the Whole World in His Hands." Jackson also worked for equal rights for African Americans.

Quincy Jones (1933–   ) of Chicago is one of modern music's most talented artists. As a composer, conductor, and trumpeter, he has won more awards than any other musician of his time. Jones helped write the song "We Are the World" and produced Michael Jackson's *Thriller* album.

Michael Jordan (1963–   ) is considered by many to be the world's greatest athlete. Raised in North Carolina, Jordan was drafted by the Chicago Bulls in 1984. He helped the Bulls win three basketball championships in a row. His exciting style of play earned him the nickname "Air" Jordan.

Jackie Joyner-Kersee (1962–   ) is considered one of the world's top female athletes. Born in East St. Louis, Joyner-Kersee has won a number of gold medals in track and field events at the world olympic games.

Ray Kroc (1902–1984) of Chicago got the idea for a restaurant that served only hamburgers, french fries, and milkshakes from two California brothers named McDonald. He opened his first McDonald's in Des Plaines in 1955. From there, a chain of restaurants spread around the world. Today, Hamburger "U," where McDonald's trains its managers, is located in Oak Brook.

Abraham Lincoln (1809–1865) moved from Indiana to New Salem, Illinois, at age twenty-one. After studying law, Lincoln moved to Springfield and opened his own law office. He served one term in the U.S. House of Representatives in the 1840s. He gained much fame through his debates with Stephen A. Douglas whom he opposed in an unsuccessful bid for a U.S. Senate seat in 1858. In 1860, Lincoln was elected the sixteenth president of the United States. After leading the North through the Civil War, he was assassinated only days after the war's end.

Marlee Matlin (1965–   ), the first deaf person to win an Oscar for an acting role, was born in Morton Grove. Matlin won her Best Actress Oscar for her role in *Children of a Lesser God* in 1987. She was also the first deaf person to hold a leading role in a television series.

Carol Moseley-Braun (1947–   ) became, in 1992, the first African-American woman to be elected to the U.S. Senate. She served ten years in the Illinois House of Representatives before being chosen to serve in the U.S. Congress. Moseley-Braun was born in Chicago.

Bill Murray (1950–   ), the popular comedian and actor, was born in Evanston. Murray came into the national spotlight with his role on *Saturday Night Live.* From television, he moved on to movies and starred in *Ghostbusters, Scrooged,* and *Groundhog Day.*

Walter Payton (1954–   ) is pro football's most successful running back. Born in Mississippi, Payton was drafted by the Chicago Bears in 1975. "Sweetness," as he was known, spent all thirteen of his pro years with the Bears, and helped them win the Super Bowl in 1985. Payton holds the record for most rushing yards by a pro running back.

Richard Peck (1934–   ), a noted children's writer, was born in Decatur. Peck's books for young adults cover sensitive issues such as suicide, pregnancy, and the death of a loved one. His books include *Remembering the Good Times* and *Ghosts I Have Been.*

Ronald Reagan (1911–   ), who became the fortieth president of the United States, was born in Tampico. Reagan grew up in Dixon and attended Eureka College before moving to California and a career in acting. He served as governor of California before being elected president.

Roseanne (1952–   ), one of America's favorite television actresses, was born in Moline. Starting out as a standup comedienne, Roseanne moved to television and her show became a huge hit. She has also starred in several feature films.

Mike Royko (1932–   ) writes about Chicago and world politics in newspapers all across the country every day. Born in Chicago, Royko often addresses serious issues such as big city government in a humorous way. He received a Pulitzer Prize for his work in 1972.

Carl Sandburg (1878–1967) was born in Galesburg and much of his writing concerned Illinois and the Midwest. He is well known for his six-volume biography of Abraham Lincoln and a number of poems including "Chicago," which gave the city its nickname, "The City of the Big Shoulders."

Shel Silverstein (1932–   ) from Chicago is famous for his popular children's books including *A Light in the Attic, Where the Sidewalk Ends,* and *The Giving Tree.* Silverstein writes and illustrates his books.

Harold Washington (1922–1987) was born in Chicago and became that city's first

African-American mayor. Washington served for many years in the Illinois legislature and then in the U.S. House of Representatives before being elected Chicago's mayor in 1983. He worked to bring women and minorities into city government.

Robin Williams (1952–   ) of Chicago has become one of America's best-loved comedians and actors. Known for his impersonations and zany style of comedy, Williams has appeared in many films including *Hook, Dead Poets Society,* and *Mrs. Doubtfire.*

Oprah Winfrey (1954–   ) was born in Mississippi. In 1984, Winfrey accepted a job at a Chicago television station. Her talk show quickly became popular and before long was being seen all across the nation. Winfrey went on to star in movies, such as *The Color Purple,* and she is today one of America's wealthiest women.

TOUR THE STATE

Ulysses S. Grant Home State Historic Site (Galena) The people of Galena gave this house to Grant when he returned following the Civil War. It contains some of the Grants' original belongings.

John Deere Historic Site (Grand Detour) This historic site includes Deere's restored home and a reconstructed blacksmith shop.

Starved Rock State Park (La Salle) Starved Rock rises 125 feet (38 meters) into the air and is so named in memory of the group of Illinois Indians who made their last stand there and were wiped out because they lacked food and water.

Blackberry Historical Farm Village (Aurora) This reconstruction of an Illinois farm includes guides dressed in period costume and a Discovery Barn with farm animals.

McDonald's Museum (Des Plaines) The museum is built on the site of the original 1955 restaurant and tells the story of the popular eating place.

Brookfield Zoo (Brookfield) This large zoo holds mammals, reptiles, and birds in cageless areas that resemble their natural habitats.

Hull House (Chicago) Jane Addams' famous settlement house has been restored; exhibits found inside show the history of the neighborhood.

Chicago Children's Museum (Chicago) This fun museum has exhibits on garbage and Legos.

The Field Museum (Chicago) This huge natural sciences museum contains exhibits on everything from gems to ancient Egypt to dinosaurs.

John G. Shedd Aquarium (Chicago) More than six thousand freshwater and marine animals, including whales and dolphins, can be found here.

Sears Tower (Chicago) Visitors to the world's tallest building can view the city from the observation deck on the 103rd floor.

Lincoln's New Salem Historic Site (Petersburg) The town where Abraham Lincoln lived from 1831–1837 is reconstructed at this site.

Lincoln Home National Historic Site (Springfield) The house found at this location is the only home Lincoln ever owned.

Lincoln's Tomb State Historic Site (Springfield) Mrs. Lincoln and three of the four Lincoln children are also buried in this beautiful monument.

Illinois State Museum (Springfield) Three floors of exhibits showcase Illinois' natural history as well as the history of the state's Native Americans and settlers.

Giant City State Park (Carbondale) Huge blocks of stone rise from the canyons of this rugged park.

Fort de Chartres State Historic Site (Prairie du Rocher) The stone buildings at this site are an imitation of those found in the 1760s when Fort de Chartres was a French settlement in the Illinois country.

Cahokia Mounds State Historic Site (Collinsville) Cahokia Mounds is the site of a city inhabited by Indians of the Mississippian culture from A.D. 900–1500. Sixty-five mounds still exist, the largest standing over one hundred feet tall.

Reenactment of the Fort Massac encampment, Metropolis

Cahokia Courthouse State Historic Site (Cahokia) The courthouse was built in 1737 as a French home and is the oldest building in Illinois.

Joseph Smith Historic Center (Nauvoo) Several buildings related to the town's Mormon past are found at this site.

Fort Crevecoeur Park (Peoria) A reconstruction of the fort built in 1680 by La Salle near a Peoria Indian village is found here.

Wildlife Prairie Park (Peoria) Bison, elk, wolves, and bears can be seen on the two thousand acres (eight hundred hectares) of preserved prairie found here.

Mississippi River Visitor Center (Rock Island) Visitors can watch as boats pass through the locks on the Mississippi and learn a lot more about river travel.

FUN FACTS

One lesser known nickname for Illinois is the "Sucker State." No one is sure where this name came from. Some people think it goes back to the days when Illinois was just being settled. Crawfish in the area burrowed into the ground, creating small holes that often filled up with fresh water. Pioneers could then suck up the water from the holes, which they called suckers.

On September 10, 1890, a shower of fish fell on the town of Cairo. No explanation has ever been given for the event.

The pinball game was invented by Chicago's In and Outdoor Games Company in 1930.

Robert Wadlow, born in Alton in 1918, was the tallest man in the world. Wadlow stood 8 feet, 11 inches tall, weighed 491 pounds (although he looked thin), and wore a size 37 shoe.

FIND OUT MORE

If you'd like to find out more about Illinois, look in your school library, local library, bookstore, or video store. Here are some titles to ask for:

GENERAL STATE BOOKS

Fradin, Dennis. *Illinois.* Chicago: Childrens Press, 1994.

Marsh, Carole. *Illinois Quiz Bowl* Crash Course. Decatur, GA: Gallopade Publishing, 1992.

Stein, Conrad. *Illinois.* Chicago: Childrens Press, 1987.

Wills, Charles. *The Historical Album of Illinois.* Brookfield, CT: Millbrook Press, 1994.

SPECIAL ILLINOIS PEOPLE AND INTEREST BOOKS

Beaton, Margaret. *Oprah Winfrey: TV Talk Show Host.* Chicago: Childrens Press, 1990.

Bial, Ray. *Portrait of a Farm Family.* New York: Houghton Mifflin, 1995.

Bial, Ray. *Visit to Amish Country.* New York: Houghton Mifflin, 1995.

Brooks, Gwendolyn. *Children Coming Home.* Chicago: Gwendolyn Brooks, 1991.

Cumpían, Carlos. Latino Rainbow. Chicago: Childrens Press, 1994. (biographies in verse about well-known Latinos, including many Illinoisans)

Kent, Deborah. *Jane Addams and Hull House.* Chicago: Childrens Press, 1992.

Macy, Sue. *A Whole New Ball Game.* New York: Henry Holt, 1993. (about the women's baseball league)

Marsh, Carole. *Illinois Pirates, Bandits, Bushwackers, Outlaws, Crooks, Devils, Ghosts, Desperadoes, Rogues, Heroes, and Other Assorted & Sundry Characters.* Decatur, GA: Gallopade Publishing, 1990.

Sandburg, Carl. *Rootabaga Stories. The Sandburg Treasury: Prose and Poetry for Young People.* New York: Harcourt Brace Jovanovich, 1956, (selections from biographies of Sandburg and Abraham Lincoln and poems about Illinois).

VIDEOTAPES

"Michael Jordan Come Fly With Me." New York: CBS Fox Video Sports, 1989.

"Illinois Historic Panorama, Overview." Macomb, IL: WIU/ISBE Satellite Education Network, Western Illinois University, 1991.

COMPUTER DISKS/AUDIOTAPES

"Route 66." David Williams. Chicago: Warehouse Hotel Music Publishing, 1995. (songs about Chicago and the Mississipi River)

"Jim Post and Friends." Galena: URDU (FL) Indpendent, 1993. (songs about Galena and the Mississippi River valley)

INTERNET

On the Internet, go to the State of Illinois Home Page at www.state.il.us on the World Wide Web. You will find pictures, information, and suggestions for further research about the state.

INDEX

Page numbers for illustrations are in boldface.